THE PÈRE MARQUETTE
LECTURE IN THEOLOGY
2000

IS THE REFORMATION OVER?

GEOFFREY WAINWRIGHT

MARQUETTE
UNIVERSITY
PRESS

BX
4818.3
.W35
2000

Library of Congress Cataloguing-in-Publication Data

Wainwright, Geoffrey, 1939-
  Is the Reformation over? : Catholics and Protestants at the
turn of the millennia / Geoffrey Wainwright.
     p. cm. — (The Père Marquette lecture in theology ;
2000)
Includes bibliographical references.
  ISBN 0-87462-580-7 (alk. paper)
  1. Catholic Church—Relations—Protestant churches.
  2. Protestant churches—Relations—Catholic Church.
I. Title. II. Series.
  BX4818.3 .W35 2000
  280'.042—dc21

                                                    00-008412

Copyright © 2000
Marquette University Press
Milwaukee WI 53201-1881

Manufactured in the United States of America

Member, Association of American University Presses

Marquette University Press
MILWAUKEE

The Association of Jesuit University Presses

Foreword

The annual Père Marquette Lecture in Theology commemorates the missions and explorations of Père Jacques Marquette, S.J. (1637-75). The 2000 lecture is the thirty-first in the series begun in 1969 under the auspices of the Marquette University Department of Theology.

The Joseph A. Auchter Family Endowment Fund has endowed the lecture series. Joseph Auchter (1894-1986), a native of Milwaukee, was a banking and paper industry executive and a long-term supporter of education. The fund was established by his children as a memorial to him.

Geoffrey Wainwright

In a recent *Festschrift* honoring Geoffrey Wainwright on the occasion of his sixtieth birthday he received personal congratulatory greetings from the Ecumenical Patriarch, Bartholomew of Constantinople; the Prefect of the Sacred Congregation for the Doctrine of the Faith, Joseph Cardinal Ratzinger; and the Archbishop of Canterbury, George Carey. That a Methodist minister would be so recognized gives a hint of the wide esteem in which he is held on all sides of the ecumenical world not to mention his "crucial contributions to the World Methodist Council that have brought [it] integrity and strength" as acknowledged by its General Secretary, Joe Hale. As teacher, scholar, churchman and ecumenist, Wainwright has made his mark for more than three decades in the effort to achieve visible Christian unity.

Born in 1939 in the West Riding of Yorkshire, England, Geoffrey Wainwright was reared in British Methodism. Although his theological interests would soon become apparent he began his studies in Modern Languages at Cambridge University, a talent that has served him well in establishing his international reputation with publications in several languages. After completing his B.A. at Cambridge in 1960 (followed by an M.A. there in 1964), he was accepted for candidacy in the British Methodist Church in 1961, studied at Wesley College, Headingly (1962-64) and served on the probationary circuit until ordained to the presbyterate in 1967. His pastoral appointment during this period was in the Liverpool suburbs (1964-66) and was a joint Methodist/Anglican one which fit well with his emerging ecumenical associations in Rome, Geneva and the World Council of Churches. He received the B.D. degree from Cambridge in 1972 (a D.D. in 1987) and the D.Théol. from the University of Geneva in 1969 with studies at the Waldensian Faculty of Theology in Rome (1966-7).

Professor Wainwright's service in the Academy began as Professor of Systematic Theology at the Faculté de Théologie protestante at Yaoundé, Cameroun (1967-1973) followed by six years at Queen's College, Birmingham (1973-1979). He then arrived in the United States when he was called to the Roosevelt Chair of Systematic Theology at Union Theological Seminary in New York

(1979-1983). His present position beginning in 1983 as holder of the Robert Earl Cushman Chair of Christian Theology at the Divinity School of Duke University returned him to his Methodist roots (albeit the United Methodist Church in the U.S.) and introduced him to the American south.

Although collegial recognition of Geoffrey Wainwright's contribution to theological scholarship is well in evidence, it is service to the cause of Christian unity for which he is best known. In regard to the former he exercised leadership during his presidencies of the international Societas Liturgica (1983-85) and the American Theological Society (1996-97). He has also served on the editorial boards of *Studia Liturgica* (as editor, 1974-87), *One in Christ* (1975-present), *Pro Ecclesia* (advisory council, 1991-present), *Ex Auditu* (1988-present) and *Studies in Historical Theology*, Labyrinth Press, Oxford University Press (1984-present). Ecumenical service landed him on the Faith and Order Commission of the World Council of Churches from 1977 to 1991 during which he chaired the final edition of the Lima text of 1982, *Baptism, Eucharist and Ministry*. This document has been instrumental in forging further ecumenical convergence among the churches. He also chairs the World Methodist Council's Committee on Ecumenism and Dialogue and is presently co-chair of the international Methodist-Roman Catholic Dialogue as well as a member of the Council's commissions with the Anglican communion and the Orthodox Churches.

Geoffrey Wainwright's legacy will long remain through his many books and articles (some 270 titles!) and among the students he has mentored and influenced. The heart of Wainwright's theological work and perspective remains his 1980 book *Doxology: The Praise of God in Worship, Doctrine and Life*. Preceded by his landmark study *Eucharist and Eschatology* and followed by collections of essays and books edited on ecumenism, liturgy and Methodist identity in the Church catholic, Wainwright had plied his original insights into the constructive theological value of the ancient axiom, "*Lex Orandi, Lex Credendi*" (the law of prayer is the law of belief). Hence more recent works such as *Geoffrey Wainwright on Wesley and Calvin: Sources for Theology, Liturgy and Spirituality* (1987) and *For Our Salvation: Two Approaches to the Work of Christ* (1997) reveals Wainwright's ability to fruitfully engage different theological traditions and models to manifest the rich texture of Christian faith borne along in the worship of the church.

It is with all this in mind that we present this lecture mindful that for Geoffrey Wainwright no end is more desired in Christian service than that proffered by his ancestor in the faith, John Wesley, who at the close of his sermon on "The New Creation" states (and quoted by Wainwright in *For Our Salvation*): "To crown all, there will be a deep, an intimate, an uninterrupted union with God; a constant communion with the Father and his Son, through the Spirit; a continual enjoyment of the Three-One God, and of all the creatures in him."

Ralph Del Colle
The Feast of the Presentation of the Lord

Is the Reformation Over?

Catholics and Protestants
at the Turn of the Millennia

Augsburg 1999

On October 31st 1999, in Augsburg of Bavaria, representatives of the Lutheran World Federation and of the Pontifical Council for Promoting Christian Unity signed a Joint Declaration on the Doctrine of Justification that was hailed by the secular press as bringing to an end almost half a millennium of division in Western Christendom. The fracture that an Imperial Diet held in that same city had failed to halt and heal in the year 1530 was now considered mended, and the solemn signing took place (what's more) on All Saints' Eve, the date on which Martin Luther had affixed his Ninety-Five Theses to the door of the castle church in Wittenberg of Saxony and which had in the intervening centuries been kept in the Protestant calendar as Reformation Day. Since Luther himself—or Lutherans close to him—had regarded justification as the "articulus stantis et cadentis ecclesia," a genuine agreement on this point might well, at least to Lutherans, appear to allow Lutherans and Catholics to stand together in a single Church.[1]

In theological and ecclesiastical reality, however, the matter was not as simple as the journalism of the sound-bite and the photo-op presented it. For, on the Lutheran side itself, the Joint Declaration had been viewed as substantially inadequate by some 150 German professors of theology who, "in discharge of their responsibility for theology and church," had in 1998 formulated a statement of their dissatisfaction that was apparently not entirely assuaged even by the "annex" appended to the Joint Declaration in June 1999 whereby the Roman Catholics also now recognized the propriety of the contested phrase "sola fide" that had been avoided in the original document.[2] Moreover, the authority for the Lutheran World Federation to speak and act on behalf of the constitutionally autonomous Lutheran churches was also called into question. Then, on the Catholic side, too, it had been made evident that justification was not the single issue that determined the ecclesial status of a community, and that differences on such matters as (say) eucharistic doctrine, or episcopal succession, or the authority of the Bishop of Rome, continued to forbid that intercommunion between the Lutheran and Catholic bodies which for some Lutherans ought to have been the immediate—and perhaps finally sufficient—result of agreement on justification (supposing it had been reached).

The step taken at Augsburg on October 31, 1999, was therefore more modest than the world's information media made out, but its significance remains great and its consequences may prove vast.[3] Technically, what occurred was that Catholics and Lutherans each formally stated that the official anathemas that they had cast at one another in the sixteenth century—without necessarily naming names—did not strike the present teaching on justification given by the two bodies respectively, as that teaching was now formulated in the Joint Declaration. That teaching was epitomized in a common formulation in paragraphs 15-17 of the Joint Declaration and then unfolded in twenty-one further paragraphs of "differentiated consensus" where the distinctive confessional nuances were retained but seen as "bearable" within the basic agreement; further "clarifications" were offered in the "annex" to "substantiate" the statement. We shall have to come back later to the doctrine of justification; but meanwhile it should already be obvious that it is impossible to return a simple answer of "Yes" to the question of whether the Reformation is over, while a resounding "No" would also be untrue to the considerable achievements of the ecumenical twentieth century.

Before unpacking the rather complex potentialities of our question, however, it may in fact be useful to offer a bird's-eye view of the century just ended. That exercise may not be so necessary for those of us who lived through most of that century and even participated actively in one of its great ecclesiastical movements; but when I taught a guest semester at the Gregorian University in 1995, I kept having to remind myself that most of my students had not even been born at the time of the Second Vatican Council, whose course I had myself followed closely as a budding ecumenist during my years as a Methodist seminarian and then as a young pastor in Liverpool, England.

THE ECUMENICAL CENTURY

The ecumenical century did not begin that way, at least as far as relations between Catholics and Protestants were concerned.

In its early decades, the ecumenical movement was at first an affair among Protestants.[4] Springing from evangelistic concerns in the late nineteenth century, the modern ecumenical movement is conventionally dated from the World Missionary Conference held at Edinburgh, Scotland in 1910. Mere cooperation among the sending agencies and the practice of comity in the overseas fields were not sufficient to the task of "the evangelization of the world in this generation": both at home and abroad, leaders with a deeper vision saw that the existence of confessional and institutional division constituted a counter-testimony to the Gospel of reconciliation. Bishop Charles Brent, a missionary of the Protestant Episcopal Church to the Philippines, was inspired by Edinburgh 1910 to propose a movement of Faith and Order that would tackle the questions of doctrine, worship and pastoral structures that separated the churches. In 1920, an initiative came from the Orthodox side, when the Ecumenical Patriarchate of Constantinople published an encyclical letter "to the churches of Christ everywhere" proposing, by analogy with the incipient League of Nations, a "fellowship of churches" that would foster rapprochement among them through study and co-operation and enable them to bear witness together in face of the social consequences of World War I. Simultaneously, the Swedish Lutheran archbishop Nathan Söderblom began preparing for the Universal Christian Conference on Life and Work that would take place in Stockholm in 1925 and carry forward the movement for "practical Christianity" devoted to the concerns of freedom, peace, and justice in national and international affairs. By 1927 the Faith and Order movement was ready to hold its first world conference, at Lausanne in Switzerland, with a strongly Protestant composition but also some participation from the Hellenic Orthodox churches. The International Missionary Council, founded in 1921, held its first world conference at Jerusalem in 1928, although the Orthodox churches always remained wary of this entirely Protestant body on account of suspected proselytism. Nevertheless, by the end of the 1920s the three movements that would eventually coalesce in the World Council of Churches were up and running: "Faith and Order" and "Life and Work" provided the principal constituency for the inaugural assembly at Amsterdam in 1948, and the integration of the International Missionary Council with the WCC occurred at New Delhi in 1961.

Where were the Roman Catholics while all this was going on? Between 1921 and 1925, the Malines conversations took place discreetly between Catholics and Anglicans at the initiative of the high-church English Anglican layman, the second Viscount Halifax, and under the presidency of Cardinal

Mercier of Belgium; but the proposal "L'Eglise anglicane unie, non absorbée" fell on deaf ears. In 1928, Pius XI's encyclical *Mortalium Animos* forbade Catholics to participate in ecumenical gatherings for fear of religious "indifferentism"; instead, the Pope pleaded for "the return to the one true Church of Christ of those who are separated from it." The ecumenical engagements of Catholics remained for a long time tentative and unofficial, often courageous though always ambiguous because of the flavor of Romanocentrism that ecclesiologically attached to them. The "spiritual ecumenism" of Paul Wattson (1863-1940) and Paul Couturier (1881-1953) encouraged prayer for unity "as Christ wishes and by the means he wishes." Pioneering theological work was done by Yves Congar in his *Chrétiens désunis* (1937).[5] Congar in fact was one of a number of Catholic scholars whose writings— though often viewed with suspicion by Roman authorities—contributed to what might be called an "academic ecumenism" in the areas of Bible, patristics, historiography, and liturgy and provided in the years after the Second World War the intellectual foundations for the surprising event of the Second Vatican Council (1962-65).

Permit me to illustrate by personal anecdote the ecumenical change wrought by Vatican II. When I was an undergraduate at Cambridge in the late 1950s, the only religious act that we were officially allowed to undertake together as Protestants and Catholics was the recitation of the Lord's Prayer; even that was a recent concession for Catholics, and then we never knew whether to continue with "For thine is the kingdom, the power, and the glory…" As a graduate student at the WCC's Ecumenical Institute of Bossey near Geneva in 1963-64, I joined in an informal series of weekend exchanges set up by some English Benedictines who were studying at the University of Fribourg and have maintained to this day friendships begun at that time. I spent the year 1966-67 in Rome while writing my doctoral dissertation, was admitted to libraries that usually guarded their reading privileges closely, was received by Paul VI in a limited audience of theological students, and was invited several times to ordinations in the Sistine Chapel. During my time as a missionary in Cameroon, West Africa, from 1967 to 1973, our Protestant Faculty of Theology at Yaoundé developed the most cordial relations with the Engelberg Benedictines of Mont Febé, where we established an Ecumenical Study Circle. Similar practices occurred between the Queen's College, Birmingham, where I taught from 1973 to 1979, and the Catholic seminary of Oscott College, England. Since 1983 I have been a member—and since 1986 the co-chairman—of the Joint Commission between the Roman Catholic Church and the World Methodist Council. Our vigorous theological work in this bilateral dialogue is sustained by common prayer, and we all attend the eucharist as celebrated respectively by both partners in the dialogue, though we do not share at each other's Table.

The key ecumenical document from Vatican II was, of course, the decree *Unitatis redintegratio*. The decree on ecumenism recognized that other Christians are, by faith in Christ and the baptism that signifies it, set in some measure of communion, albeit imperfect, with the (Roman) Catholic Church; and that, while the one Church of Christ "subsists in" the (Roman) Catholic Church, other churches and ecclesial communities—defective though they may be in some matters of doctrine, sacraments, and order—are nevertheless "not without significance and importance in the mystery of salvation." Explicitly included are those communions, "national or confessional," that were separated from the Roman see during "the grave crisis that began in the West at the end of the Middle Ages" and as a result of "the events which are commonly referred to as the Reformation." The "dialogues" encouraged by Vatican II have characteristically taken a bilateral form, and the Protestant partners in international conversation with the Roman Catholic Church under the aegis of the Secretariat (later Pontifical Council) for Promoting Christian Unity have been the Anglican Communion, the Lutheran World Federation, the World Methodist Council, the World Alliance of Reformed Churches, the Disciples of Christ, and the difficult-to-define "Evangelicals." While the Roman Catholic Church has not joined the World Council of Churches, there has existed ever since Vatican II a Joint Working Group for official consultations between the Roman Catholic Church and the World Council of Churches; and since 1968 the Roman Catholic Church has had twelve appointed members of the 120-strong WCC Commission on Faith and Order.

In his encyclical of 1995, *Ut unum sint*, Pope John Paul II reiterated the "irrevocable" commitment of the Roman Catholic Church to ecumenism and affirmed the common obligation of all Christians to evangelization. He recognized the considerable amount of doctrinal agreement achieved so far by Faith and Order and the bilateral dialogues and looked for further progress on the basis of "Sacred Scripture as the highest authority in matters of faith" and "Sacred Tradition as indispensable to the interpretation of the Word of God" (a formulation that offers the greatest promise for a settlement of principle on a matter of fundamental controversy since the sixteenth century). The Pope also acknowledged the "effective presence" of "the one Church of Christ" beyond Roman Catholic boundaries (opening a more attractive perspective for others on reunion than that of a simple "return" to Rome) while at the same time offering the see of Rome as a universal "ministry of unity" to be exercised in ways that should be the object of further dialogue. To these matters we shall come back later.

After that sketch of the institutional history of the twentieth-century ecumenical movement, with its special focus on Protestants and Catholics, we must face up to our main question: "Is the Reformation over?" That question itself may be heard in several different ways. The idea might be that the Roman Catholic Church has now, for good or ill, accepted the proposals by which Luther launched the Reformation. Alternatively, it could be argued that Protestant truth has sold out to Rome or, to construe the matter from the other end, that Protestantism is on the point of being welcomed back into the Catholic fold. A third, and more irenical possibility would be that the unfortunate mutual "misunderstandings" of the sixteenth century have at last been cleared up. Or again, the sixteenth-century controversies may be thought to have been real and important enough in the intellectual and cultural circumstances of their time but to have since become irrelevant or at least no longer church-dividing. Fifth and finally, it might be considered that genuine and substantial differences, which were insoluble when they first arose, can now be reconciled and overcome through the discovery of new insights into the Gospel and the faith or (more likely) through the recovery of more original perceptions that antedate the Reformation. It is according to this fivefold grid that I will now tackle the titular question, using each time some deliberately over-sharp phraseology in the sub-titles. I shall try to match the different versions of the question with doctrinal issues where there is at least some *prima facie* plausibility in formulating the question that way.[6]

HAS THE CATHOLIC CHURCH TURNED PROTESTANT?

Archbishop Marcel Lefebvre judged that, with Vatican II, the Catholic Church had indeed turned Protestant. The sign of it was "the new Mass":

> It is obvious that this new rite is, if I may put it this way, of an opposing polarity, that it supposes a different conception of the Catholic religion, that it supposes a different religion. It is no longer the priest who offers the Holy

Sacrifice of the Mass, it is the assembly. Now this is a complete program. From now on it is also the assembly which will replace authority in the Church…. It is the weight of numbers which will give the orders from now on in the Holy Church. And all this is expressed in the Mass precisely because the assembly replaces the priest, to such an extent that now many priests no longer want to celebrate the Holy Mass if there is not an assembly there. Very quietly, it is the Protestant idea of the Mass which is creeping into Holy Church. And this is in accordance with the mentality of modern man, with the mentality of modernist man, completely in accordance, for it is the democratic ideal which is fundamentally the idea of modern man. That is to say that power in the assembly, authority is invested in men, *en masse*, and not in God…. This Mass is no longer a hierarchic Mass, it is a democratic Mass.[7]

Archbishop Lefebvre was so convinced of the infidelity of the post-Vatican II church that he ordained bishops to serve the communities of the truly faithful and thereby brought upon himself excommunication from the Roman see.

It might be more Catholic to see Protestantism as having helped the Roman Church to recover what is, as Yves Congar saw at the time, an authentically traditional notion of the baptismal priesthood of the faithful. Certainly Pope John Paul II followed and strengthened that line in his apostolic exhortation *Christifideles Laici* that completed the Synod on the Laity of October 1987.[8] There, baptism itself gives the commission to share in Christ's triple ministry to evangelize, sanctify, and serve—a ministry that laypeople have the special responsibility of exercising "in the world." Moreover, these sentiments do not require that either Pope John Paul or a classical Protestant should acquiesce in Lefebvre's caricature of Protestantism in its own weakest manifestation, as though the Church were an internally undifferentiated community in which all authority was self-generated "from below"—or in the rank individualism for which the liberal newspaper columnist Susanna Rodell awarded Martin Luther the accolade of "person of the millennium."[9]

Certainly there are signs that the Roman Catholic Church has ceased to oppose a thing simply because Protestants affirm it, or to maintain it simply because Protestants reject it. In this sense, Vatican II may have signaled, as an ecumenical German study suggested, "the end of the Counter-Reformation."[10] Thus the guarded opening which the Council gave to the use of the vernacular has in fact led almost to the abandonment of the Latin Mass in ordinary practice. The homily, too, has been made an integral part of the eucharist ("*pars ipsius liturgiae*"), so that the old contrast no longer obtains, at least on the Catholic side, between Protestantism as "the church of the Word" and Catholicism as "the church of the Sacrament" (though Protestants for their part have hardly yet caught up with the program of Luther, Calvin, and the English Reformers for a full service of the Lord's Supper on every Lord's Day).[11] Or again, lay communion under both kinds has become quite widespread among Catholics (though one may wonder whether the intinction hygienically fashionable in some Protestant circles would itself meet Luther's insistence on "drinking the cup" in accordance with the Lord's institution).[12]

Nevertheless, a married priesthood is not yet conceded in the "Latin" rite of the Roman Catholic Church, despite the marginal exceptions made for men already having been ordained as Protestant pastors. Of greater doctrinal significance is the fact that the practice of indulgences, though it has become much more discreet, has not disappeared. The matter flared up again with the papal bull of November 1998 setting the terms for the Holy Year of 2000 and led to the withdrawal of the World Alliance of Reformed Churches from the ecumenical commission linked to the Roman Committee of the Jubilee. Protestants find it difficult to square the forgiveness of sin by grace through faith with a subsequent remission of temporal penalty according to a tariff for specified works. Whether indulgences can be accommodated within the agreement between Lutherans and Catholics on justification remains to be seen; and we shall need to return to the related, though distinguishable, matter of purgatory among the topics on which further reflection is needed.

Clearly, then, the Catholic Church has not "turned Protestant" in any facile sense, even while it has at last met some of the concerns of the magisterial Reformers. In fact, such a suspicious Protestant as one of my old teachers—Vittorio Subilia, the great dogmatician late of the Waldensian Faculty of Theology in Rome—concluded that, by accepting *selected* elements of the Protestant position, the "new catholicity of Catholicism" was playing the old

Catholic trick of integrating them into a "complex of opposites" … and thereby neutralizing them.[13]

Might it even be, Subilia used to wonder, that sympathetic but incautious Protestants were allowing themselves to be taken in by the ancient adversary? Indeed, enough of my own former students have by now swum the Tiber that colleagues ask whether I am receiving a commission. The second version of the question "Is the Reformation over?" must therefore be formulated: Has Protestantism poped?

HAS PROTESTANTISM POPED?

Vittorio Subilia characterized Catholicism as the religion of the "and." This he drew from the "*et*" of the Council of Trent's decree on "Scripture *and* Tradition." But it was also a question of faith *and* works, of Christ *and* the Church. Original Protestantism, said Subilia, held to an "either/or." At stake were the Reformation watchwords of the *sola Scriptura*, the *sola gratia* and the *sola fide*, and the *solus Christus*. Thus Methodism, for instance, with its version of justification *and* sanctification, represented a decline;[14] and Subilia would doubtless have agreed with the Belgian Franciscan Maximin Piette in his Louvain dissertation that the Wesleyan movement constituted a catholic "reaction" in the evolution of Protestantism.[15]

A bugbear for those who see themselves as the defenders of pure Protestantism lies in what they detect as any tendency towards "sacramentalism." They bring out the Reformers' polemic against the *opus operatum* understood in terms of the *opus operantis*, as though the ministers of the rite were supplementing the work of Christ. The charge of sacramentalism was leveled against the Lima text of Faith and Order on *Baptism, Eucharist and Ministry* in a number of responses from Protestant churches, often in combination with an accusation of neglecting or subordinating "the Word."[16] Whereas Orthodox churches typically charged that *BEM*, by its use of the category of "sign," was reducing the sacraments to mere "pointers," some Protestant responses feared that altogether too much "efficacy" was being attributed to the ritual performance. The Church of North India captured a wider sense of unease when it remarked on the fact that "transitive verbs like 'unites,' 'makes,' 'initiates,' 'gives' are used with baptism as the subject" and proposed that such statements should be reworded in such a way that God or Christ or the Holy Spirit becomes the subject;[17] and while Faith and Order later clarified that the meaning was indeed "God through baptism,"[18] it seems unlikely that this will have calmed the more extreme Protestant disquiet.

In all this question of "catholicizing" tendencies, the Strasbourg Lutheran André Birmelé probably probed most deeply to the neuraligic point when, after his thorough and extensive survey of "Salvation in Jesus Christ according to the Ecumenical Dialogues" (1986), he isolated the question of the instrumentality of the Church: it is a matter of whether the Church has a role in mediation (*Vermittlung*) that goes beyond the "simple communication" (*Mitteilung*) of the Gospel. In so far as

Catholic theology allows, and Catholic doctrine affirms, an active role of the Church (as when Vatican II in *Lumen Gentium*, 64 taught that "by preaching and baptism the Church gives birth to children whom she has conceived by the Holy Spirit"), it is running foul of the crucial Lutheran doctrine of justification understood in its sheer passivity.[19] It will be interesting to see whether the Joint Declaration on Justification of 1998-99 permits this point to be resolved.[20]

WERE THEY MERE MISUNDERSTANDINGS?

In his great work *Die Reformation in Deutschland*, which was published as the Second World War was starting and which eventually launched a much more positive phase in the Catholic historiography of Protestantism, Joseph Lortz argued that Luther both was influenced by and rebelled against an Ockhamism which obscured the true nature of Catholicism.[21]

That line was pursued by other authors, both Catholic and Protestant (particularly Anglican), to explain and excuse the Reformers' rejection of the sacrifice of the Mass. The then-Jesuit Francis Clark, in *Eucharistic Sacrifice and the Reformation* (1960),[22] caused that little apple-cart to tremble for a while by showing that a pure line of Catholic teaching persisted from the middle ages to the Council of Trent (namely, that the sacrifice of the Mass and the sacrifice of Calvary are one and the same sacrifice, so that there can be no question of repetition or addition of a pelagian or works-righteousness kind), and by arguing that the Reformers' destruction of the Mass was, *in consequence*, done with open eyes. In turn, Nicholas Lash, a fellow Catholic, charged Clark with greatly underestimating the complexity of the relationship between verbal orthodoxy and the practical context: "If what the Church is doing, in the concrete, can reasonably be said to be significantly different from what she ought to be doing" (and Clark admitted the practical abuses prevalent in the late medieval period), then (said Lash) "the theory according to which she interprets her activity may be calculated to mislead, even if that same theory, when employed as the interpretation of a more adequate state of concrete activity, were irreproachable."[23] J. F. McCue had gone even further: "When theologians who defend the sacrificial concept of the Mass seem not to be disturbed by the development of a sub-Christian understanding of sacrifice within Roman Catholic piety, then there is at least some justification for thinking that the piety does express the doctrine."[24] On my reckoning, the question of eucharistic sacrifice is better placed among the issues that were awaiting the rediscovery of a primitive category.

The controversies over justification form another area in which the diagnosis of misunderstanding has been proposed for peace-making purposes. In the original edition of his book *Rechtfertigung* (1957), the young Catholic theologian Hans Küng argued that Karl Barth had "misunderstood" the Tridentine decree on justification, and that there was in fact a fundamental agreement between Barth's position and that of the Catholic Church. By the time of the first English edition (1964), Küng was stressing in his preface that remaining differences were "school differences," where "misunderstandings" are notoriously prevalent. In the new English edition of 1981, Küng went so far as to say that the "anathemas pronounced by the Council of Trent against the Reformation doctrine of justification were based on misunderstanding and lack of understanding, that is, they were mistaken decisions like so many others in the course of history" (pp. xvii-xviii); though, admittedly, such writings of Luther's as *The Bondage of the Will* and *On Good Works* "were and are open to misunderstanding, in need of completion and correction, not infallible."[25]

Still in the area of justification, the Catholic dogmatician Otto Hermann Pesch has invoked "misunderstanding" in regard to the two sub-themes of certainty of salvation, and faith and works.[26] Concerning faith and works, Pesch speaks simply of "the most superfluous of all controversies." On the other topic, Pesch claims that in rejecting certainty of *eternal* salvation, the Council of Trent was reverently drawing a line between the incomprehensible Creator and human pride and fickleness; Luther, on the other hand, was rightly preaching *present* certitude which accompanies trust in the reliable word and redemptive grace of God. For Luther, faith—which is of course the fruit of grace—*includes* love towards God and *expresses itself* in good works; whereas Catholic language tends to take faith as intellectual assent and in *that* sense sees it in need of "supplementation."[27]

Three decades of post-Vatican II dialogue have brought Lutherans and Catholics to their Joint Declaration on the Doctrine of Justification. Their "common understanding" deserves full quotation in view of our overall interest in the current relations between Catholics and Protestants:

> 15. In faith we together hold the conviction that justification is the work of the triune God. The Father sent his Son into the world to save sinners. The foundation and presupposition of justification is the incarnation, death, and resurrection of Christ. Justification thus means that Christ himself is our righteousness, in which we share through the Holy Spirit in accord with the will of the Father. Together we confess: By grace alone, in faith in Christ's saving work and not because of any merit on our part, we are accepted by God and receive the Holy Spirit, who renews our hearts while equipping and calling us to good works.
> 16. All people are called by God to salvation in Christ. Through Christ alone are we justified, when we receive this salvation in faith. Faith is itself God's gift through the Holy Spirit who works through word and sacrament in the community of believers and who, at the same time, leads believers into that renewal of life which God will bring to completion in eternal life.
> 17. We also share the conviction that the message of justification directs us in a special way towards the heart of the New Testament witness to God's saving action in Christ: it tells us that as sinners our new life is solely due to the forgiving and renewing mercy that God imparts

as a gift and we receive in faith, and never can
merit in any way.

On that basis and within that framework, the Joint
Declaration proceeded to "explicate" the doctrine in
relation to seven historically controversial points. In
each case a common confession is made, which is
then followed by a paragraph from each side in
which the respective positions of Catholics and
Lutherans are stated in such a way as also to ward
off—what is particularly interesting for our present
discussion—the apparent *mis*understanding to which
their interlocutors had hitherto subjected them. As
a single example of this pattern we may take what is
said about "human powerlessness and sin in relation
to justification":

> 19. We confess together that all persons depend
> completely on the saving grace of God for their
> salvation. The freedom they possess in relation
> to persons and the things of this world is no
> freedom in relation in relation to salvation, for
> as sinners they stand under God's judgment and
> are incapable of turning by themselves to God
> to seek deliverance, of meriting their justifica-
> tion before God, or of attaining salvation by
> their own abilities. Justification takes place solely
> by God's grace. Because Catholics and Lutherans
> confess this together, it is true to say:
> 20. When Catholics say that persons "cooper-
> ate" in preparing for and accepting justification
> by consenting to God's justifying action, they
> see such personal consent as itself an effect of
> grace, not as an action arising from innate
> human activities.

> 21. According to Lutheran teaching, human beings are incapable of cooperating in their salvation, because as sinners they actively oppose God and his saving action. Lutherans do not deny that a person can reject the working of grace. When they emphasize that a person can only receive (*mere passive*) justification, they mean thereby to exclude any possibility of contributing to one's own justification, but do not deny that believers are fully involved personally in their faith, which is effected by God's Word.

What seems to be occurring here is a recognition that, within certain limits, differing positions—on (say) the relative activity and passivity of the human person in salvation—need not, when properly and fairly *understood*, figure as theologically incompatible. There remains, however, a distinct awkwardness in the fact that one partner continues to use the word "cooperate" affirmatively while the other partner continues to deny it.[28] And with that we almost come to the fourth variation of the question "Is the Reformation over?": Is the truth—or at least its formulation—variable with time and place? Crudely put: Does doctrine (still) matter?

DOES DOCTRINE (STILL) MATTER?

While Yves Congar sympathized with Luther's contention that the Gospel itself creates its own language,[29] Otto Herman Pesch went so far as to suggest that Luther's *new experience and understanding* of the Gospel made it (practically) inevitable that "the old believers" would condemn the new linguistic expression which it appropriately found.[30] But if

indeed Luther's teaching was condemned by the
Council of Trent (and while on the one hand Luther
was not named by Trent, yet on the other hand the
Joint Declaration of 1999 refers only to the present
teaching of the Lutherans as not struck by the
Tridentine anathemas), then it is difficult to see how
a Church which invests such magisterial authority in
a general council could now admit precisely "Luther's
Gospel" as a "Catholic possibility." And that is
precisely the point made by Pesch's fellow-Catholic
critics when he first made the proposal: Can what
was error in the sixteenth century become true in the
twentieth?[31] And yet it was not only Pesch who was
ready to call Luther a "doctor of the Church," but
Pesch's Catholic critic Peter Manns admitted Luther
as a "father in the faith," while Cardinal Willebrands,
then president of the Secretariat for Promoting
Christian Unity, spoke of Luther as "our common
teacher."[32] What was going on?

It was such developments as these that stimulated
George Lindbeck to write his much discussed book
The Nature of Doctrine, although the book ranged
far beyond its ecumenical occasion and provoked a
broad discussion on "religion and theology in a
postliberal age."[33] Lindbeck had been an observer on
behalf of the Lutheran World Federation at the
Second Vatican Council and subsequently served as
a co-chairman of the bilateral dialogue between the
LWF and the Roman Catholic Church. He knew at
first hand the phenomenon of "reports from Roman
Catholic, Orthodox, or Protestant theologians engaged in dialogues sponsored by their respective
churches that they are in basic agreement on such

topics as the Eucharist, ministry, justification, or even the papacy, and yet they continue—so they claim—to adhere to their historic and once-divisive convictions."[34] To make such cases intelligible, Lindbeck proposed what he called "a 'regulative' or 'rule' theory" of "church doctrine": doctrines— abstraction made of any purported cognitive content—function as "communally authoritative rules of discourse, attitude, and action."[35] Superficial oppositions between rules may at least sometimes be resolved "by specifying when or where they apply, or by stipulating which of the competing directives takes precedence." A prerequisite for successful resolutions—it is implicit in Lindbeck's proposal—is that a common intention underlies the particular rules that appear to conflict. But it is hard to pin Lindbeck down as to whether such a substratum may or must have substantive content or is rather itself simply a regressive "rule" which may be treated independently of its propositional truth or falsity.

The difficulty with Lindbeck's regulative theory of doctrine becomes evident in his very subtle discussion of the Marian dogmas of Roman Catholicism concerning the Assumption and, especially, the Immaculate Conception of Mary: he seeks to show how, at the formal level, "a regulative approach leaves the theological options open and is therefore capable of accommodating irreversibility as well as reversibility (not to mention the usual Protestant view, which the rule theory also allows, that these doctrines are simply illegitimate)."[36] But it appears inadequate, as an attempted settlement of the material differences between the confessions, to note that

the Eastern Orthodox did not develop a doctrine of
Mary's immaculate conception because the precon-
dition of an Augustinian doctrine of original sin was
not present in the East, while parts of the West
developed this Marian doctrine and others did not,
even though they all for long shared Augustine's
teaching (but perhaps were unequal in their piety
towards Mary). As Lindbeck himself notes (and it is
obvious here that he hedges concerning the material
content versus the merely formal character of "the
rules" that he had wished to maintain): "One could
view the Immaculate Conception as a valid application in particular circumstances of permanently
essential rules.... [Only] it is ... difficult [in this
case] to specify what the underlying rules might be.
One might have to content oneself with saying that
they have to do with the uncodifiable aspects of the
interaction of divine and human freedom. Further-
more, although the positive affirmation of the Immaculate Conception would be temporary or
reversible, it could still be maintained that it is
irreformably wrong to assert the negative: that Mary
was born in original sin. This, indeed, would be
meaningless, because it is the traditional Western
notion of original sin which has become problem-
atic. Thus the reason this doctrine [of the Immaculate Conception] can be easily understood as reversible
is that some of the rules involved in its emergence
(viz., those connected with a particular theology of
sin) seem themselves to be temporary."[37]

Now, there is great value in Lindbeck's general
reading of Christianity as a cultural tradition and
community whose speech and practices need to be

taught and learned. But in my estimation, this is precisely the context in which the nature of Christian truth requires that language and substance be held together, *pace* Lindbeck, in *cognitive propositions* which hitherto divided churches may together affirm.

Whereas Lindbeck was chiefly concerned with the diachronic changeability of doctrines, it was the question of their synchronic variability that came to the fore in the scheme proposed by Karl Rahner and Heinrich Fries for making the reunion of the churches "a real possibility."[38] In 1983, the two veteran Catholic theologians, dogmatician and ecumenist respectively, put forward eight theses, the first two of which are crucial to our discussion. First, "the basic truths of Christianity, as they find expression in Holy Scripture, in the Apostles' Creed, and in the Nicene-Constantinopolitan Creed, are to be binding upon all particular churches (*Teilkirchen*) in the future united Church." And second, "realistically": "In no particular church may there be a deliberate and confessional rejection of any position that is a binding dogma in another particular church. But neither may any church be required to make an explicit and positive confession of a dogma from another particular church"—though such an issue may become the object of a more developed consensus in the future. The overall proposal envisaged a quite stable continuation of existing confessional bodies, even on the same territory and even while each became open to the history and experience of those from which it had been separated. While "pulpit and altar fellowship" would exist between

the continuing bodies (thesis 8), the immediate
result, at least, would be a "diversity" that was
scarcely "reconciled" in any substantive sense. What
would hold the churches together would be "the
Petrine ministry of the Roman Pope as the concrete
guarantor of the unity of the Church in truth and
love" (thesis 4); but in fact, the question of truth
risked being downplayed in the Rahner-Fries proposal. Doctrinally, the whole scheme seemed to
depend on the view, expounded by Rahner in com-
menting on thesis two, that within—but also despite—the common framework of the Scriptures
and the Creeds, the contemporary explosion and
fragmentation of knowledge has rendered to a large
degree "incommensurable" the theological options
not only of individuals but also of social groups and
even confessional communities, so that a rather
broad "epistemological tolerance" is not only inevitable but justified even on quite substantive matters.
But the question must be raised, of just how wide a
pluralism of theological interpretation may become
before it sinks into dogmatic indifferentism.

In my judgment, then, it will by now be clear: while
the doctrinal discussion in Faith and Order and in
the bilateral dialogues will not be sufficient by itself
to unite the churches, it is necessary work; and it has
indeed some impressive accomplishments to its credit.
It is with these in mind that I pose our titular
question in its fifth and most positive form: Are
matters now settled?

ARE MATTERS NOW SETTLED?

Are doctrinal matters between Catholics and Protestants now settled? The appropriate answer is: More than they were.

Here I want to give four examples of categorical rediscovery that have begun to unlock some genuine and substantial controversies between Protestants and Catholics in ways that open the door to doctrinal agreement and thence to reunion. These keys may be labeled "Gospel," "Memorial," "Communion," and (here's perhaps the novel one) "Trajectory."

1. Gospel

In New Testament usage, exegetes have retaught us, "gospel" designates both the material content and the active proclamation of the one saving message. This gets behind the question of Scripture and tradition to their common source. It is significant that Vatican II dropped the preparatory draft on "the two sources of revelation" and produced instead, in *Dei Verbum*, a document which allows the "*et*" of Trent to be taken—according to a possibility which J. R. Geiselmann and others have argued was always meant to be left open—as treating Scripture and unwritten tradition in the sense of two mutually interactive ways of transmitting and testifying to the one Gospel.[39] At the same time, the WCC Conference on Faith and Order at Montreal in 1963 produced its text on Scripture, the great Tradition (with a capital T), and the particular traditions (plural, and with a small t): the traditionary process is that by which "the Gospel itself," "testified in Scripture," is "transmitted in and by the Church through the power of the Holy Spirit," "actualized in the preaching of the Word, in the administration of the Sacraments and worship, in Christian teaching and theology, and in mission and witness to Christ by the lives of the members of the Church."[40]

Clearly, not everything was theoretically settled by *Dei Verbum* and Montreal: Montreal recognized the need for "a criterion" in evaluating the sometimes divergent traditions in the interpretation of canonical Scripture; and *Dei Verbum* attributed to the "living Magisterium" a role which Montreal regarded as characteristically—and, by implication, controversially—Roman. Nevertheless, the convergence of theoretical perspectives was sufficient to allow material convergences in the areas of "Baptism, Eucharist and Ministry" and suggest such in the still continuing study—in which Catholic theologians also participate as full members of Faith and Order—"Towards the Common Expression of the Apostolic Faith Today."[41] These ongoing achievements, partial as they are, are not only important in themselves but also lend concretion to the further fundamental study which, as we shall see, Pope John Paul considers necessary on the relation between "Sacred Scripture" and "Sacred Tradition" in the cause of a unity in truth which belongs both to the substance and to the spread of the Gospel.

2. Memorial

Twentieth-century biblical and patristic scholarship has also delivered to us a more ancient understanding of the notion of "memorial." When, at the Last Supper, Jesus instituted the eucharist with the command "Do this in remembrance of me," he could presuppose the Israelite practice of the Passover as the remembrance of the Exodus: behind the *eis tên emên anamnêsin* of 1 Corinthians 11:24-25 stands the *le-zikkaron* of Exodus 12:14 and 13:9 and much other phraseology with the root *ZKR* in the Old Testament.[42] Despite some differences of detail in exegesis and interpretation, it is now widely agreed that a ritual or liturgical memorial, in the Scriptures, is a God-given means of putting succeeding generations in contact with the original and normative events in which revelation and redemption were given; or, as I put it when as chairman of the drafting group I introduced the text of *Baptism, Eucharist and Ministry* to the full Faith and Order Commission at Lima in January 1982, a memorial is "a word, act or rite given to us by God, as a command and a promise, to put us in touch, by the Holy Spirit, with the saving activity of God which is being commemorated."[43]

The biblical category of memorial, often explicated in terms of "efficacious representation," has already allowed for a considerable substantive convergence—after four centuries of controversy—between Catholics and Protestants in their doctrinal understanding of Christ's presence and the sacrificial character of the eucharist. In light of the original text of *BEM* and the churches' responses to the Lima document it was thus possible to declare: "The Lord's Supper is neither the occasion of a simple mental recollection of Christ and his death, nor yet a repetition of Calvary. It is rather a means graciously given by Christ himself for the realization of his presence. In the Holy Spirit, Christ comes to us, clothed in his mighty acts, and gathers us into his self-offering to the Father, in whom is eternal life."[44]

Yet not everything is thereby settled. While generally strong endorsement was given by the churches to the formulation of *BEM* concerning "Christ's real, living, and active presence in the eucharist," not all considered that differences over the relation of that presence to the elements of bread and wine could be "accommodated within the convergence formulated in the text," and the Roman Catholic response in particular considered that justice had not been done to what was meant by transubstantiation.[45] Similarly, the Roman Catholic response reckoned *BEM*'s talk of a sacrifice of praise, thanks, and intercession inadequate to the Catholic doctrine, although many of the Protestant responses had shown grave reservation over any kind of sacrificial language at all.[46]

Still, the notion of "memorial" gave biblical backing to the twentieth-century understanding of Christ's death and resurrection as the "paschal mystery" into which Christians are taken through baptism and eucharist. This understanding—viewed with suspicion at first because the pioneering work of Dom Odo Casel emphasized rather the analogies in hellenistic religion—shaped much liturgical revision in both Catholic and Protestant churches in the last third of the twentieth century, and the use of current service-books will lend concretion to the further theological work that needs to be done with a view to greater convergence and even consensus in sacramental doctrine.[47]

3. Communion

The notion of "communion"—*koinônia*—received much attention in both biblical and systematic scholarship in the second half of the twentieth century, especially perhaps from theologians with an ecumenical interest and commitment. Thus my own Methodist mentor Raymond George wrote an exegetical study on *Communion with God in the New Testament* as early as 1953, and the Orthodox dogmatician Metropolitan John Zizioulas's *Being as Communion* (1985) proved a landmark in the rediscovery of the Trinity among systematicians.[48] Having long been around as a category in official ecumenism, *koinônia* achieved new prominence with the Fifth World Conference on Faith and Order at Santiago de Compostela in 1993 which was held under the title "Towards Koinonia in Faith, Life and Witness."[49]

A strongly tri-personal understanding of the Blessed Trinity allows the Godhead to be treated as not only the origin but also the model of ecclesial unity in communion, and indeed its goal. Just as Vatican II's dogmatic constitution *Lumen Gentium*, citing St. Cyprian, saw the Church as "a people brought into unity from the unity of the Father, the Son and the Holy Spirit,"[50] so the decree on ecumenism, *Unitatis Redintegratio*, spoke of "the sacred mystery of the unity of the Church, in Christ and through Christ, with the Holy Spirit energizing its various functions. The highest exemplar and source of this mystery is the unity, in the Trinity of Persons, of one God, the Father and the Son in the Holy Spirit."[51] Mary Tanner, future moderator of Faith and Order, addressed the 1983 Vancouver Assembly of the World Council of Churches in these terms:

> The Church must take its identity from the God in whom it seeks to live, the Triune God whose nature and being mysteriously allows for unity and diversity. The identity of the sign [which the Church is for the world] becomes sure only as the Church finds its unity in the *fellowship* of the Son with the Father into which the Holy Spirit takes it (John 17:21). As the Church participates more deeply in the life of the Trinity, as in the process of renewal it is drawn more deeply into the eternal divine *fellowship*, so the human face of the Church will be conformed to the Triune God and bear God's image for the world.... The Triune God provides a model for unity in that ever-flowing mutual love and indwelling [among the persons of the Trinity]; but much more than model, for the Triune God is the very ground of the Church's unity. The Church is only an authentic sign to the world when, overcoming brokenness and division, it allows itself to be drawn into and enfolded in the unity of Father, Son and Holy Spirit and discovers its true identity.[52]

To give an example from a Catholic-Protestant bilateral dialogue, the Joint Commission of Methodist and Catholics was so taken by the notion of "communion" (*koinônia*) that it placed as an exordium to its 1991 Singapore report on *The*

Apostolic Tradition a paragraph from its own 1986
Nairobi report, *Towards a Statement on the Church*:

> Because God so loved the world, he sent his Son
> and the Holy Spirit to draw us into communion
> with himself. This sharing in God's life, which
> resulted from the mission of the Son and the
> Holy Spirit, found expression in a visible
> *koinonia* [communion, community] of Christ's
> disciples, the Church.

Since 1986, the Catholic-Methodist international
commission has repeatedly declared the aim of the
dialogue to be "full communion in faith, mission
and sacramental life."

The biblical and patristic category of *koinônia* has
certainly provided inspiration, method, direction,
and objective for Catholics and Protestants in nego-
tiating the mending of their fractures. Of clear
benefit is the value it gives to "spiritual ecumenism"—
the appearance together before the triune God in
prayer and in common receptivity towards God's
gifts—in the face of any reduction of the search for
ecclesial unity to the merely legal or institutional
level. But it is precisely at this point that the incom-
pleteness of the present relations between Catholics
and Protestants emerges most acutely. For on the
question of *communicatio in sacris* there is a characteristic difference of principle concerning the nature
of communion—or at least a characteristic difference of prudential judgment concerning the condi-
tions of sacramental communion between churchly
bodies not fully reconciled to one another. While
most Protestant theologians and communities in the

modern ecumenical movement have considered "intercommunion" an appropriate stage in the convergence of hitherto separated bodies towards fuller unity, the Roman Catholic Church—though making since Vatican II a few pastoral exceptions for individuals—has rather, like the Orthodox Church, viewed eucharistic communion as a part of the goal which must not be pre-empted.[53]

Another question of communion that remains unresolved is that of the relation between the local church and the Church universal. The matter is not uncontroversial even on Roman Catholic terrain, as the 1992 Letter of the Congregation for the Doctrine of the Faith on "The Church as Communion" made evident.[54] As between Catholics and Protestants, the caricatural opposition between a Protestant tendency to "congregationalism" and a Roman inclination to view the dioceses or parishes as branch offices of a central corporation may be mitigated by a eucharistic ecclesiology that, in the words of the Swiss Reformed theologian Jean-Jacques von Allmen, views the local church as "wholly Church, but not the whole Church."[55] But that still leaves open the question of the pastoral and governmental structures by which the local churches are bound together.

That brings us to one of the historically controverted matters on which the fourth, and perhaps fairly novel, categorical insight may offer help. The possibly helpful notion is that of "trajectory."

4. Trajectory

Again, it is scholars of the primitive and early Church who have supplied us with the hermeneutically useful concept of a "trajectory." Certain lines of historical and doctrinal development—the use of the word hints that the insight may go back to John Henry Newman and even beyond—can be shown to have at least their beginnings in the normative apostolic period. No doubt they open up a considerable vector of possibilities, only some of which were actually realized in later history, though perhaps more of them remain theologically open. In particular, the U.S. Lutheran-Roman Catholic dialogue in the 1970s used the notion of trajectory in connection with Peter and with Mary.[56]

Thanks chiefly to the presence of the exegete Raymond E. Brown, insights from the U.S. Lutheran-Catholic dialogue were taken up—an example, by the way, of the frequent cross-fertilization among the dialogues—by the international Catholic-Methodist commission in its 1986 Nairobi Report, entitled with appropriate tentativeness *Towards a Statement on the Church*. Noting the "distinctive church-oriented role" attributed to Peter in the gospels and beyond, the report points to the leadership of this "first" among the apostles in his own time (*prôtos*, Matthew 10:2) and hints at his prototypical status for what Catholics at least see as a continuing "Petrine" ministry:

> The New Testament depicts Peter in a plurality of images and roles: missionary fisherman (Lk. 5:1-11; Jn. 21:1-14); pastoral shepherd (Jn.

21:15-17; Lk. 22:32; 1 Pet. 5:1-4); witness and martyr (1 Cor. 15:5; cf. Jn. 21:18-19; 1 Pet. 5:1); recipient of special revelation (Mt. 16:17; Acts 10:9-16; 2 Pet. 1:16-18); the "rock" named by Jesus (Mt. 16:18; Jn. 1:42); recipient of the keys of the kingdom of heaven (Mt. 16:18); confessor and preacher of the true faith (Mt. 16:16; Acts 2:14-40); guardian against false teaching (2 Pet. 1:20-21; 3:15-16; Acts 8:20-23); and weak human being and repentant sinner, rebuked by Christ and withstood by Paul (Mk. 8:33; Mt. 16:23; Mk. 14:31, 66-72; Jn. 21:15-17; Gal. 2:5). Most of these images persist through two or more strands of the New Testament tradition, and several recur in subsequent Church history.[57]

More recently, Walter Klaiber, the German Methodist bishop and a New Testament scholar, has recognized in the scriptural texts a "*Verständnispotential*" for a continuing Petrine ministry; but as a theologian he considers that that "potential" would have to be judged not in light of the development of the Roman see and its claims over the centuries but rather in light of the total message of Jesus; and as a practical ecumenist, he wonders whether the "monumentality" of the existing papal office would not prevent the development of a differently conceived Petrine ministry.[58] Other Protestants might question, more starkly, whether it would ever be possible to reconcile the very checkered "history of the popes" with an office which in principle transcends its holders in a ministry of permanent and universal significance. We shall, however, look on the brighter side when we return shortly to the matter of the Petrine ministry.

In their work on Mary, the American Lutherans and Catholics found, on the basis of the "relatively slight" material, that "in the New Testament and in second-century literature the mother of Jesus was pictured in ways that were not uniform and, in some cases, not harmonious." Nevertheless, they were able to trace "some lines of development which were increasingly positive in portraying Mary as a disciple par excellence and as the virgin. In later centuries these positive lines dominated and were greatly enhanced." As Marian piety unfolded "with a momentum of its own," Christians "saw Mary's role in the wider context of the divine history of salvation," and thus took further the "Marian symbolizing within the Church" to which the door had been opened by (say) the Fourth Evangelist's own symbolic treatment of Jesus' mother at the foot of the cross (John 19:25-27) or by the typology of the "virgin Eve" and the "virgin Mary" that Justin Martyr and Irenaeus already found it easy to extend from the Pauline typology of the first and second Adam in Romans 5:12-21.[59]

A quarter-century ago, in an essay on "Mary and Methodism," I myself made a modest attempt to look back from a later point in Christian history and ask whether some characteristic emphases in my own ecclesial community could not be set in relation to the historic and dogmatic Mary in such a way as to facilitate for Methodists a sympathetic understanding of Catholic teaching and practice in regard to her. With careful qualifications I suggested, for instance, that the Methodist sense of faith as "active receptivity" might find a correspondence in Mary's "*fiat*" at the Annunciation; that the Methodist stress on "entire sanctification" might illuminate the meaning of Mary's immaculate conception and her assumption; and that Methodism's insistence on the universal offer of the Gospel might not be out of harmony with Mary as the mother of a new humanity.[60] My arguments must have failed to persuade some Methodists, to judge by the kerfuffle among the executive committee of the World Methodist Council, seated in places of honor at a papal audience in September 1997, when Pope John Paul pursued his catechetical series on Mary "with Methodists present."

Things, then, and not just the Marian questions, are not yet fully settled between Protestants and Catholics. John Paul II himself recognized as much when, in his encyclical *Ut Unum Sint* of 1995, he identified five areas "in need of fuller study before a true consensus of faith can be achieved"; and such a consensus is needed, said the Pope, because "the obligation to respect the truth is absolute."[61] The Pope's list comprised (1) Scripture and Tradition, (2) the eucharist as sacrament, sacrifice, and sanctification, (3) sacramental ordination to the threefold ministry, (4) the papal and episcopal magisterium, and (5) Mary. Let us now look at the prospects in each of those areas.

Scripture and Tradition

I have already revealed my hand in declaring as the most promising opening towards a settlement of principle John Paul's formulation of the issue as that of "the relationship between Sacred Scripture, as the highest authority in matters of faith, and Sacred Tradition, as indispensable to the interpretation of the Word of God."

Such a Catholic acknowledgment of the supremacy of Scripture ought to satisfy Protestants who, once they get beyond a sloganeering comprehension of "*sola Scriptura*," realize that Scripture is never in fact "alone" but is always read within a diachronic and synchronic community of interpretation for which it remains, of course, a permanent and unsurpassable norm (as Catholics must also admit). Moreover, for classical Protestants at least, the Apostles' Creed and the conciliar Creed of Nicea, Constantinople, and Chalcedon—precisely, of course, in their perceived fidelity to Scripture—have always been taken as the irreversible deliverances and continuing guides of the Tradition in its interpretation of Scripture. It is *within* this relationship between Scripture and Tradition that the question of the teaching office in the Church must be considered, for, as Vatican II recognized in paragraph 10 of *Dei Verbum*, "this Magisterium is not superior to the Word of God, but its servant; it teaches only what has been handed on to it." We shall come to the Magisterium in a moment.[62]

Meanwhile, a couple of broad scholarly tasks may be indicated which could help to concretize work

between Catholics and Protestants towards a consensus on Scripture and Tradition. First, one might
envisage mixed groups of Protestants and Catholics
implementing the program implied in the Lutheran
Gerhard Ebeling's conception of "Church history as
the history of the interpretation of Holy Scripture."[63] Detailed study might, for instance, test and
nuance the common reading of "the apostolic tradition" that was attempted by the Catholic-Methodist
international commission in its 1991 report under
that title, and in particular might help to keep a
scriptural norm functioning in the scarcely yet
broached task of a common understanding and
evaluation of the rise of Methodism in the history of
the Gospel, and therefore of the place of Methodist
communities in the Body of Christ. Yves Congar
recalled the challenge of the question once put to
him by a Catholic student at Strasbourg: What is the
meaning of the Reformation in God's plan?[64] Catholics and Protestants should be seeking a common
answer in the light of Holy Scripture.

Second, and in a complementary movement, com-
ing at the question of Scripture and Tradition not
now from the angle of Church history but from the
angle of the Scriptures themselves: there would be
value in common studies that traced the way in
which particular books or passages of Scripture have
been interpreted in the Tradition. This process
would reveal, for instance, what elements had been
stable in traditional interpretation, and the manners
of interaction between canonical text and change-
able contexts of time and place. It might encourage
the revival of certain approaches to Scripture that

had more recently become eclipsed but could now once more enrich the appropriation of the sacred writings in the life of the Church. The growing scholarly interest in the fourfold sense of Scripture—literal/historical, allegorical/doctrinal, moral, and anagogic/mystical-eschatological—could be put to ecumenical use in virtue of the fact that it antedates the confessional and institutional divisions, in much the same way as a common return to patristic principles facilitated the revision of liturgies along convergent lines in the latter half of the twentieth century.[65]

An opportunity for bringing the ecumenical treatment of Scripture and Tradition into the very heart of parish life is afforded by developments in lectionary use. The Roman *Order of Readings for Sunday Mass* was taken as the basis for a *Common Lectionary* (1983; revised 1992) that is now very widely employed in many Protestant churches throughout the English-speaking world.[66] It may not be beyond the bounds of possibility that the Roman Church, having seen its lectionary so gratefully received in some other communities, would in turn welcome it back with the relatively minor suggestions for improvement that have been made and tried; this would not be the first case of such a to-and-fro in liturgical history (as study of the medieval sacramentaries shows), and the result would be an even closer ecumenical convergence in Sunday Scriptures. Even now, preachers are often able to prepare their messages together, and congregations to receive God's Word in a uniting way.[67]

THE EUCHARIST

The second area identified by the Pope for fuller study towards consensus was "the Eucharist, as the Sacrament of the Body and Blood of Christ, an offering of praise to the Father, the sacrificial memorial and Real Presence of Christ, and the sanctifying outpouring of the Holy Spirit."

I hope it was not accidental that the sequence of John Paul's eucharistic themes here corresponds to the structure of the section on "Eucharist" in Faith and Order's *Baptism, Eucharist and Ministry* (1982). In expounding "the meaning of the eucharist," *BEM* begins with the forthright declaration that "the eucharist is essentially the sacrament of the gift which God makes to us in Christ through the power of the Holy Spirit. Every Christian receives this gift of salvation through communion in the body and blood of Christ. In the eucharistic meal, in the eating and drinking of the bread and wine, Christ grants communion with himself." Then, in a trinitarian structure, the eucharist is treated as "thanksgiving to the Father" ("the great sacrifice of praise"), as "anamnesis or memorial of Christ" ("the memorial of the crucified and risen Christ, i.e. the living and effective sign of his sacrifice, accomplished once and for all on the cross and still operative on behalf of all humankind," in which "Christ himself with all that he has accomplished for us and for all creation ... is present"), and as "invocation of the Spirit" (where "the whole action of the eucharist has an 'epikletic' character because it depends on the work of the Holy Spirit," and "the Church, as the community of the new covenant, confidently invokes the Spirit, in order that it may be sanctified and renewed, led into all justice, truth and unity, and empowered to fulfil its mission in the world"). I am confident that the Pope would not quibble with *BEM*'s decision to expand the trinitarian pattern—as the Creeds do— by subjoining the ecclesiological and eschatological themes of the eucharist as "communion of the faithful" and as "meal of the Kingdom."

This structure was widely approved in the responses of the churches to the Lima text, and it surely provides the trinitarian and salvation-historical framework within which to pursue closer agreement on the historically controversial points of Christ's presence and sacrifice. Moreover, the categories of "anamnesis" and "epiklesis"—especially when taken together—were widely regarded as promising avenues of progress.

On "Christ's presence, its mode, and especially its relation to the elements of bread and wine," Faith and Order synthesized the responses of the churches thus:

> It would be quite contrary to the overwhelming tradition of Christianity, and to the scriptures as there interpreted, to hold that the bread and wine had no part in Christ's presence at the Lord's supper. On the other hand, no church holds that Christ's eucharistic presence is limited to the bread and wine: Christ is present in the assembly gathered for prayer in his name (Matt. 18:20; Col. 3:16), in the reading of the scriptures which bear testimony to him (John 20:31), in the proclamation of the gospel con-

cerning him (Luke 10:16; Rom. 10:17), and in the hearts of believers (Gal. 2:20; Col. 1:27). It is within this universe of meaning that any ecumenical confession of Christ's presence must be made.

It is also generally believed that the presence of the crucified and risen Christ at the supper is a pneumatic presence, a presence by the power of the Holy Spirit. That is common ground. It may be agreed, too, that Christ's presence is a mystery, in the sense that it cannot happen except for the sheer grace of God.

As the subject for continuing dialogue, Faith and Order then declares it important that "the Roman Catholic Church explore with others how what is 'most aptly called transubstantiation' (Council of Trent) may otherwise be expressed," and that "those Protestants who deny any 'essential change' in the elements state what they are thereby affirming."[68] Regarding sacrifice, Faith and Order proposed the following to the churches in a second go-round after the churches' responses to *BEM*:

Christ "offered himself to God through the eternal Spirit" (Heb. 9:14). Christ now "ever lives to make intercession for us" (Heb. 7:25). When Christ, in instituting the eucharist on the eve of his passion, commanded his followers to "do this in remembrance of me, *eis tên emên anamnêsin*," he delivered the bread with the words "this is my body," and the cup with the words "this is my blood of the new covenant" (Matt. 26:28; Mark 14:24) or "this cup is the

new covenant in my blood" (Luke 22:20; 1 Cor.
11:25).

All churches affirm that Christ's sacrifice is
unique—sufficient, unrepeated, unsupple-
mented. All affirm that the church is, by the
Spirit, graciously included in the access which
Christ's sacrifice gives to the Father (Eph. 2:18).
All agree that the benefits of Christ's saving
work are gratefully received in and by communion, made possible by the Holy Spirit (cf. 2 Cor.
13:14). All agree that, in Christ, Christians are
to present themselves, body and soul, as a living
sacrifice to God, consecrated by the Holy Spirit
(Rom. 12:1f.; 1 Cor. 6:11, 19).

It is, then, within such a firm and massive agreement at the level of confessed faith that Faith and
Order then simply records that "different theological expressions and visions are used in various traditions in order to relate the order of sign and sacrament
in the eucharist to the unique sacrifice of Christ."[69]
It is, of course, up to the churches to decide just how
far they wish to push for agreement in the
theologoumena.

Again, to keep the continuing dialogue close to the
heart of the practical life of the churches, I would
urge that Catholics and Protestants with some regu-
larity be present at—and, as far as their disciplines
allow, participate in—the eucharistic celebrations of
their conversation partners. As *BEM* affirmed, "Christian faith is deepened by the celebration of the Lord's
Supper" (E 30), and it would be appropriate that this
deepening take place in a common and convergent
way among Protestants and Catholics. As a Protes-

tant, I am committed to the pastoral recovery of the principle enunciated by John Wesley as "the Supper of the Lord on every Lord's Day."

ORDINATION

John Paul II's third area identified for further study was "ordination, as a sacrament, to the three-fold ministry of the episcopate, presbyterate and diaconate."

Regarding the sacramentality of ordination, it may first of all be noted that almost all classically Protestant churches do ordain to ministry in the name of Christ by the imposition of hands with prayer for the Holy Spirit.[70] What is perhaps less often noticed by Catholics is that, even among their seven sacraments, ordination is peculiar in being the only one where the act is not directly intended for personal benefit of the recipient but is immediately oriented to the service of the entire community. The adoption of a "high functionalist" view of the ordained ministry, as Raymond George used to call it, would shift the emphasis away from the ontological questions that have often weighed down the debate between Protestants and Catholics in this matter. Nor need such a view run counter to the value placed by Pope John Paul on the divine calling addressed directly by God to individual Christians, recognizing that a vocation must be tested by the Church before the introduction of a person into special ecclesial ministry; for such a vocation and ministry, even as it "configures" the minister to Christ, does so precisely for the sake of service—"a total gift of self to the Church, following the example of Christ."[71]

The threefold structure of the ordained ministry—episcopate, presbyterate, diaconate—was commended by *BEM* "as an expression of the unity we seek and also as a means for achieving it" (M 22). Except among the Reformed or Presbyterian family, this question no longer appears so controversial in ecumenically minded Protestantism. Even some churches hitherto not ordered that way, such as those in the British Methodist tradition, have more recently either moved towards that pattern on their own account or have shown their willingness to do so as part of an entrance into unity with others. But such convergence does not necessarily invalidate *BEM*'s claim that "the threefold pattern stands evidently in need of reform," listing such matters as the functions of the diaconate, the collegial dimensions of leadership, and the clarification of the relationship between presbyterate and episcopate (M 24). These are surely matters on which Catholics and Protestants can reflect together.

Episcopacy, of course, is not only a matter of synchronic structure but also raises the still controversial and delicate question of diachronic continuity. *BEM*'s description of "the episcopal succession as a sign, though not a guarantee, of the continuity and unity of the Church" proved provocative. In the context of M 38, the description occurs rather obliquely, since it appears as part of a statement of the terms on which "churches which have not retained the episcopate" are more recently expressing a willingness "to accept episcopal succession as a sign

of the apostolicity of the life of the whole Church."
Anglican evaluations of the Lima text seemed content with the phraseology of "sign, though not a
guarantee"; but the Roman Catholic response held
out for the language of "guarantee" on the grounds
that the personal figure and ministry of the bishop
sacramentally "embodies and actualizes both catholicity in time, i.e. the continuity of the church across
the generations, as well as the communion lived in
each generation," so that episcopal succession expresses "Christ's faithfulness to the church to the
end of time."[72]

Noteworthy, however, is the immediately following Catholic recognition that episcopal succession
"lays upon each individual office-bearer the responsibility to be a faithful and diligent guarantor." That
emboldens me to address also to Roman Catholics
some concluding remarks I made in putting to
Anglicans the two-edged question of whether episcopal succession was for them "a matter of dogma":
"The historic episcopate may be affirmed *in so far* as
it both fulfils its responsibilities of teaching and
maintaining the faith and remains corrigible in the
light of Scripture and the steadfast practices of the
Church by the persuasion of believers within the
community who have been well taught and bear
consistent, courageous, and sanctified testimony to
Christ. Incorrigible bishops"—I might have added
"and ineffective bishops"—"should be removed from
office."[73] I was there trying to take seriously the
growing recognition that episcopal succession is a
strand—whether an indispensable strand or not is,
of course, the question still to be resolved—in a

more complex interweaving of other strains in the preservation of the Apostolic Tradition,[74] and attempting also to signal the status of "Sacred Scripture, as the highest authority in matters of faith." With the teaching function of the episcopate we arrive at the fourth of John Paul's areas in need of further study.

The Magisterium

The Pope formulated his fourth area as "the Magisterium of the Church, entrusted to the Pope and the Bishops in communion with him, understood as a responsibility and an authority exercised in the name of Christ for teaching and safeguarding the faith."

It is with the papacy that the clash between Protestants and Catholics over magisterium comes to its sharpest expression. Often it is not clear whether Luther was attacking the institution of the papacy or its incumbent at the time, though Harding Meyer has lately recalled evidence to show that Luther would have accepted a reformed papacy.[75] In *Ut Unum Sint*, paragraphs 88-97, John Paul II invites the leaders of other churches and their theologians to engage with him "in a patient and fraternal dialogue" on the claims of the primatial Roman see to a universal ministry of unity. He notes that the subject has started to appear "as an essential theme not only in the theological dialogues in which the Catholic Church is engaging with other Churches and Ecclesial Communities, but also more generally in the ecumenical movement as a whole," and he feels his own responsibility "in acknowledging the ecumenical aspirations of the majority of the Christian Communities and in heeding the request made of me to find a way of exercising the primacy which, while in no way renouncing what is essential to its mission, is nevertheless open to a new situation."

Here I will venture to repeat a proposal which I advanced at a Roman symposium on the theme in December 1997 and which has attracted some attention then and since:

> My respectful suggestion is that the Pope should invite those Christian communities which he regards as being in real, if imperfect, communion with the Roman Catholic Church to appoint representatives to cooperate with him and his appointees in formulating a statement expressive of the Gospel to be preached to the world today. Thus the theme of the "fraternal dialogue" which John Paul II envisaged would shift from the *theory* of the pastoral and doctrinal office to the *substance* of what is believed and preached. And the very *exercise* of elaborating a statement of faith might – by the process of its launching, its execution, its resultant form, its publication, and its reception – illuminate the question of "a ministry that presides in truth and love." *Solvitur ambulando.*[76]

In point of fact, many Protestants have already in an informal way come to see in this itinerating Pope a remarkably faithful testimony borne to the Christian faith at a very difficult time in the world's history. Amid an intellectual and cultural atmosphere of fragmentation, John Paul's charismatic witness to the possibility of truth and to the dimensions of unity and universality implicit in the Gospel of redemption has enhanced his office. The combination of person and circumstances has brought us to a favorable juncture at which to reconsider, in close touch with concrete historical realities, the more theoretical questions concerning a Petrine ministry.

It must, however, be admitted that such reconsideration is likely to be burdened, at least initially, by the previous exercise of the Roman magisterium in dogmatically defining the two Marian dogmas of the immaculate conception and the assumption. With that we come to the fifth and last of John Paul's topics requiring further study, the Blessed Virgin Mary.

Mary

John Paul's fifth area concerned "the Virgin Mary, as Mother of God and Icon of the Church, the spiritual Mother who intercedes for Christ's disciples and for all humanity."

On the whole, Protestants have paid little attention to Mary's place in the history of salvation, perhaps by reaction against perceived excesses in Catholic piety. But classical Protestantism has no trouble theologically with the "*Theotokos*"—Mary as "Mother of God"—understood as principally a confession concerning Christ's incarnation. Methodists can invoke Charles Wesley's couplet:

> Being's source begins to be,
> And God himself is born,

and occasionally express this in a way that makes
Mary visible:

> Who gave all things to be,
> What a wonder to see
> Him born of His creature and nursed on
her knee![77]

In relation to the Church, Protestants may find it
easiest to look on Mary in her capacity as an exem-
plary disciple of her son. The Swiss Reformed theologian and later director of Faith and Order, Lukas
Vischer, expanded the notion a little to say that the
Church today could well find inspiration in Mary as
the humble handmaid of the Lord and servant of
humanity.[78] This is perhaps the track by which
Protestants might approach John Paul II's designa-
tion of Mary as "icon of the Church."

To speak of Mary's current "intercession" for
Christ's (other) disciples and for all humanity raises
a more general question concerning the communion
of the saints, to which we shall come in a moment.[79]
But it may be as well to signal already the likely
Protestant discomfort with the rather grotesque
image—which no less a theologian than Eduard
Schillebeeckx endorsed—of Mary as the "neck"
joining Christ the Head to the rest of his Body;[80] and
if, even in its more sober formulation, the notion of
Mary as "the mediatrix of all grace" were to be

sharpened to "co-redemptrix," that would probably be seen as Protestants as a step altogether too far.[81]

For possible convergence towards agreement between Protestants and Catholics concerning Mary, it will be important that Protestants familiarize themselves with Catholic doctrine and practice in her regard. A sympathetic study booklet, with questions for ecumenical group discussion, was produced from the British Methodist / Roman Catholic Committee in 1995 under the title *Mary, Mother of the Lord: Sign of Grace, Faith, and Holiness* and jointly published by the Methodist Publishing House and the Catholic Truth Society. Mary, it is said, can be understood as "a sign or icon of God's grace at work among us, of our graced response of faith, and of the Spirit's work of sanctification."[82]

In any case, it seems that work in this, the fifth area identified by John Paul II for further study, Protestants and Catholics will be starting much further in arrears than in the other areas, for Mary has not so far been the subject of sustained treatment in any modern international bilateral or multilateral dialogue.

Those, then, were the five topics listed by the Pope in *Ut Unum Sint*: Scripture and Tradition; the Eucharist; Ordination; the Magisterium; and Mary. Greatly daring, I would like very briefly to add three further areas: (1) the Church expectant and triumphant; (2) the doctrinal status of moral teaching; (3) the ministry of women.

The Church Expectant and Triumphant

The central doctrinal concern of the sixteenth-century Reformers was to re-assert the sole sufficiency of Jesus Christ in the work of redemption. Besides current understandings and practices concerning the Mass, other features of life in the medieval Church that appeared to place Christ's sufficiency in jeopardy included the commerce in indulgences to benefit souls in purgatory and the invocation of the meritorious prayers of the saints. Thus the Protestant Reformation also reshaped the attitudes of its adherents concerning the Church expectant and triumphant. The notion of purgatory disappeared from Protestant consciousness, and even the mildest of prayers for the departed was frowned upon; and the saints were lost from liturgical presence, at least as regards their intercessions, and even as regards their commemoration, unless a much thinned-out version of the sanctorale was kept. While various alternatives have at times come to occupy the vacuum—so deep-rooted did the concern of humans for their dead appear to be—yet modernity has been more characterized by a total sense of emptiness in the face of death, and Protestantism may even have contributed to that, as well as suffering from it. Nor have modern Catholics remained unaffected. The time may be ripe for both the Catholic and the Protestant churches to engage together in some modest rethinking in this area.

In classic Protestantism, the predominant teaching was that believers were brought by God to perfection at the moment of death and so made ready for individual judgment. The Catholic Church continued to teach that almost all needed a further period of cleansing beyond death. In one of the rare recent ecumenical treatments of this question, the English Roman Catholic-Methodist Committee noted that "theologians"—presumably Roman Catholic theologians—"know that a variety of explanations may be offered of what exactly may need to be completed, and they know that categories of time and place and the language of purifying fire may be entirely inaccurate and just part of our earthbound imaginations." In reconciling style, the study proposed this conclusion: "Methodists and Roman Catholics are united in confessing that perfect holiness is necessary before a person can see God face to face (cf. Hebrews 12:14). When a person has reached in this life a measure of holiness which falls short of perfection, then it is believed that this perfection is conferred in the transition from this life to eternal life. Granted such basic agreements, some variety of attitudes and practices may be tolerated in a united Church."[83]

A more obvious convergence may be taking place in regard to the saints and their transgenerational communion. First, Protestant theologians appear to be showing more sympathy towards the notion that if "the prayer of the righteous avails much" (James 5:16), then we may hope to be benefited by the continuing petitions of those who are in the nearer presence of God; this may even, or especially, be the avenue by which Protestants come to consider the intercessory ministry of Mary.[84] And secondly, sev-

eral Protestant churches have begun in their recent
liturgical revisions to develop what are at least com-
memorative calendars of some outstanding Christians from the past, including not only figures from
the undivided Church but also some who belonged
to "the other party" in the times of separation. Wide
welcome was given to Pope John Paul's proposal to
create an ecumenical martyrology in celebration of
the year 2000.

My suggestion is that a tremendous fillip would be
given to ecclesial reconciliation if the Catholic Church
were to adopt a number of Protestant heroes and
heroines into its official sanctorale, for that would
bestow liturgical recognition upon the communities
in whose bosom these saints grew in the Spirit of
holiness and bore their conspicuous witness to
Christ.[85] Certainly the idea of an "exchange of
saints" would merit ecumenical exploration. It should
help what the dialogue between the Roman Catholic
Church and the World Alliance of Reformed
Churches called "the reconciliation of memories."[86]

THE DOCTRINAL STATUS

OF MORAL TEACHING

The problems of principle and of substance raised
for Christian unity by divergences in ethical teaching have received little attention in dialogues between Catholics and Protestants. The main exception
has been the "agreed statement" entitled Life in
Christ: Morals, Communion and the Church that
came from the Second Anglican-Roman Catholic

International Commission in 1994. ARCIC-II looked concretely at "two moral issues on which the Anglican and Roman Catholic Communions have expressed official disagreement: the marriage of a divorced person during the life-time of a former partner, and the permissible methods of controlling conception"; and at "two other issues concerning sexuality on which Anglican and Roman Catholic attitudes appear to conflict," namely "abortion, and the exercise of homosexual relations." At the end of its work, the Commission had become persuaded that "despite existing disagreement in certain areas of practical and pastoral judgment, Anglicans and Roman Catholics derive from the Scriptures and Tradition the same controlling vision of the nature and destiny of humanity and share the same fundamental moral values."[87]

Such a statement suggests to this reader that there is both room and need for much more ecumenical reflection in the interval between the most general "vision of the nature and destiny of humanity" and the issuance of teaching on particular ethical themes, let alone the application of "practical and pastoral judgment" in individual cases. Only so may it become possible to achieve the greater doctrinal coherence in the moral dimension that is surely needed for the common witness and discipline required by ecclesial unity.

A serious start was made on such a task at a consultation held in 1996 in Chicago under the auspices of the Lutheran Institute for Ecumenical Research at Strasbourg. The tack was to bring some leading Protestant ethicists—all Lutheran except for

the Anglican Oliver O'Donovan—into theological
engagement with Pope John Paul's moral encyclicals, notably *Veritatis Splendor* (1993) and *Evangelium
Vitae* (1995).[88] Given the way in which what Gilbert
Meilaender there called "the questions of the Reformation"—Scripture, grace, justification, faith, sin,
law, freedom, nature, conscience—underlay the discussion at Chicago, it would be a valuable move to
revisit and reopen the discussion in light now of the
Joint Declaration on the Doctrine of Justification;
and the confessional range of participants on the
Protestant side could surely be broadened, as well as
the number of Catholic participants (in good standing) increased. Such initiatives could indeed be
multiplied.

THE MINISTRY OF WOMEN

It is known that both Pope Paul VI and Pope John
Paul II warned Archbishop Robert Runcie that the
ordination of women to the priesthood, and then to
the episcopate, in some provinces of the Anglican
communion was setting a new and grave obstacle to
a doctrinal agreement on the ordained ministry such
as ARCIC-I had seemed to bring closer.[89] In the last
quarter of the twentieth century, more and more
Protestant churches proceeded to the ordination of
women, especially in the Western world where the
roles of women in society at large had been changing
most rapidly; the way was perhaps easier, the further
these churches were removed from the Roman Catholic understanding of ministerial priesthood. Pope
John Paul II insisted that the Church had no author-

ity to change its constant Tradition regarding a male priesthood whose origins resided in Christ's own institution of the apostles as such: it was a matter of "theological anthropology" according to "a plan to be ascribed to the wisdom of the Lord of the universe."[90]

On the question of women's ordination, the Faith and Order text on *Baptism, Eucharist and Ministry* declared, optimistically, that "openness to each other holds the possibility that the Spirit may well speak to one church through the insights of another. Ecumenical consideration, therefore, should encourage, not restrain, the facing of this question" (M 54). Further exploration of this matter should, I suggest, seek to hold in tandem two distinguishable but related concerns: the nature of ministerial priesthood and of ordained ministry more generally, and what John Paul himself calls "the dignity of women."

Under Paul VI, the 1976 declaration of the Congregation of the Faith, *Inter Insigniores*, had advanced the "iconic" argument that the priest's position *in persona Christi* requires that the priest be male, given the principle of St. Thomas that "sacramental signs represent what they signify by natural resemblance": "In actions which demand the character of ordination and in which Christ himself, the author of the Covenant, the Bridegroom and Head of the Church, is represented, exercising his ministry of salvation—which is in the highest degree the case of the Eucharist—his role (this is the original sense of the word *persona*) must be taken by a man. This does not stem from any personal superiority of the latter in the order of values, but only from a difference of fact on the level of functions and service."[91] To strengthen the last point, John Paul II in his apostolic letter of 1994, *Ordinatio Sacerdotalis*, characteristically developed a Marian commentary on the basis of a hint that the text of 1976 had already picked up from the thirteenth-century Pope Innocent III: "The fact," John Paul wrote, "that the Blessed Virgin Mary, mother of God and mother of the church, received neither the mission proper to the apostles nor the ministerial priesthood clearly shows that the non-admission of women to priestly ordination cannot mean that women are of lesser dignity nor can it be construed as discrimination against them." Positively, the Pope went on to note that "the New Testament and the whole history of the church give ample evidence of the presence in the church of women, true disciples, witnesses to Christ in the family and in society, as well as in total consecration to the service of God and of the Gospel"; and he quoted his own apostolic letter of 1988, *Mulieris dignitatem*: "By defending the dignity of women and their vocation, the church has shown honor and gratitude for those women who—faithful to the Gospel—have shared in every age in the apostolic mission of the whole people of God. They are the holy martyrs, virgins and the mothers of families, who bravely bore witness to their faith and passed on the church's faith and tradition by bringing up their children in the spirit of the Gospel."[92]

Such insights as the Protestant churches of the West have to offer in an ecumenical exploration of this difficult question will have to draw on their experience of this "new thing" that has developed in their midst; and it may be that the test proposed by Gamaliel in other circumstances will guide the discussion (Acts 5:38-39).

*

* *

Now that we have surveyed the history of relations between Protestants and Catholics in the twentieth century and catalogued the progress that has been made as well as listing areas that require further study, we may try to discern in its most basic and comprehesive form what is at issue between the parties. It is, I suggest, a matter of the nature, identity, and location of the Church.

Fundamental Eccesiology

Over the years I have often offered to my students, tongue-in-cheek, the following rapid sketch of Church history:

> In the fifth century, the non-Chalcedonians split from the hitherto undivided Church. Then the Byzantine East broke away in 1054. The unreformed Roman Catholics were left behind in the sixteenth century, while the continental Protestants had the misfortune of being foreigners. In the eighteenth century, even the Church of England refused Wesley's mission, so that finally only Methodists remained in the body of Christ.[93]

In such a turning of the tables, Roman Catholics are
surprised to find themselves excluded from the
Church, while Methodists are astonished to discover
they are no longer simply one "denomination" among
others. At issue, of course, are two quite different
ecclesiologies: the obvious one is that which makes
the Church indivisible by considering that schism
dispatches the offending party into the void; the
other – which is also being tweaked here, albeit
implicity – is that which acquiesces in divisions to
the point of considering the fragmentation of Christianity normal.

In *Unam Sanctam*, the papal bull of 1302, Boniface
VIII declared in the face both of the Greek Church
and of political resistance in the West that it was
"altogether necessary for salvation that every human
being be subject to the Roman pontiff." That bull
was reissued by the Fifth Lateran Council in March
1517, just a few months before Luther posted his
ninety-five theses. The Roman instinct long remained to identify the Roman Catholic Church
with the Church Catholic *toute courte*. A shift came
when the Second Vatican switched the "*est*" to
"*subsistit in*" at *Lumen Gentium*, 8: "The sole Church
of Jesus Christ … subsists in the Catholic Church,
which is governed by the successor of Peter and by
the bishops in communion with him." While the
"fulness" of the Church resided in the Roman Catholic Church, the Church was not limited to those
within its institutional boundaries. The Decree of
Ecumenism recognized that other people "who be-
lieve in Christ and have been properly baptized are
put in some, though imperfect, communion with

the Catholic Church." The furthest that the Roman imagination has so far been able to reach in recognizing the ecclesial character of others was the hint in the Balamand document of 1993 between the Catholics and the Orthodox – which received, however, a mixed evaluation on both sides – that in the quest for the "re-establishment" of unity the two "sister churches" would both have to renounce their mutually exclusive claims to be the sole legitimate legatee. It remains for the Roman Catholic Church to conclude its judgment on the "significance and importance in the mystery of salvation" which Vatican II's *Unitatis Redintegratio* declares the "separated churches and ecclesial communities in the West" not to be without. The conclusion will doubtless depend on intervening history, current dialogues, and future developments.

While, as a result of the ecumenical movement, the Roman Catholic Church has been encouraged to rethink the ecclesial status of other people and communities which claim the name of Christian and *prima facie* appear to do so with some justice, it was their own dividedness which stimulated the Protestant churches to reconsider what unity required; and in the process, they came to see that the Roman Catholic Church also could not be left out of account.

The sixteenth-century Reformers did not, of course, intend to split the (Western) Church; rather, they intended precisely to reform it. But as a result of the partial character of their success or failure, divisions did in fact occur. And not only in regard to the Roman or Papal Church, but also among Protestants. These latter divisions, while on some points confessional, were also geographical in kind. As the several divisions hardened, the theological/ecclesiological principles which had at first guided the reforming thrust then turned into distinctives of particular communities. Thus the Lutheran confession of the Church as "the assembly of all believers among whom the Gospel is preached in its purity and the sacraments are administered rightly" led to a somewhat episodic view of the Church, where "event" held the priority over "institution." The Swiss Reformed respected the institutional character of the Church, but the Calvinist emphasis on predestination heightened the tension between visibility and invisibility in its composition. In later Protestantism, the pietist and evangelical "religion of the heart" could produce a Wesleyan ecclesiology of "true believers everywhere." The inbuilt tendencies to fissiparity in Protestantism allowed already the seventeenth-century Roman Catholic J.-B. Bossuet to write an "*Histoire des variations des Églises protestantes*" (1688). The subsequent centuries multiplied what Catholics could understandably call the Protestant "sects." When Dietrich Bonhoeffer—a German Lutheran who still had some sense of a single "*corpus Christianum*"—arrived in the United States in the 1930s, he was staggered to find how much "denominationalism" was taken for granted.[94]

Such differences in ecclesiological perception among the Protestant bodies naturally make for differences with regard to the goal of unity even among the ecumenically engaged. It is, I think, no accident that Lutheran ecumenists, for instance, favor a model of "reconciled diversity," Anglicans picture a "communion of communions," and Methodists toy with Albert Outler's prospect for them of "an evangelical order in the Church catholic." And where in all this fits the patristic ideal—which many earlier twentieth-century Protestant ecumenists had learned from Eastern Orthodox ecclesiology—of "all in each place"? One wonders whether there is sufficient overlap among these various visions for them to be accommodated within a pattern whereby the Bishop of Rome could meaningfully and effectively carry out a universal ministry of unity in truth and love such as John Paul II pledged to seek new ways of providing. Perhaps that very offer will help to sharpen the focus of ecumenical vision.

We have been talking rather classically about Protestantism and Catholicism, as these entities have been treated in the ecumenical movement over the latter half of the twentieth century; and the issues we have been discussing have been those customary in Faith and Order and in the bilateral dialogues between what are now usually designated the world Christian communions. At the threshold of the twenty-first century, however, it may be necessary to ask again: Which Protestants? Which Catholics?

Which Protestants? Which Catholics?

The ecclesiastical scene is changing in some ways that are bound to affect ecumenism.

First, we cannot fail to observe the decline of the "mainstream" Protestant churches, not only in Europe but also in North America. Statistics are not everything, but there is an undeniable significance in the fact, for instance, that in 1955 two thirds of all infants born in England received baptism in the Church of England, while in 1995 the proportion had sunk to one fourth. Or, to take an example from a church which reckons membership differently: the United Methodist Church in the US fell from 9.8 million members in 1979 to 8.5 million in 1999.[95] Theologically, the secular fashion of the 1960s was probably more a symptom of an underlying or impending crisis than its cause. Certainly, the erosion of practice and allegiance seems gravest in those churches which have lost the contours and confidence of the inherited faith in a transcendent and holy God who redeems sinners and builds them up for a society in eternity. The mundanity which characterizes liberal churches has prompted some of the more traditional of their members either to attempt the tension-laden task of reform and renewal from within or to move in directions which ignore (rather than overcome) the older confessional and institutional differences. Who, then, speaks for Protestantism in ecumenical dialogue? What will be left of the partners with whom the Catholic Church first took up the conversation?

Concomitant, secondly, with the decline of "mainstream" Protestantism has been the rise of the "Evangelicals." Leaving aside those who feel led to start an "independent church," we find that many Evangelicals, as hinted, stay within the churches where they "happen to be" and either seek to reform and renew them or else find their most serious Christian fellowship with soul mates in transdenominational fashion. Many Evangelicals also now make common cause with Roman Catholics on important points of faith and morals, as in the case of Evangelicals and Catholics Together.[96] On the other hand, it must be noted that many Evangelicals manifest little interest in the fuller doctrinal consensus or in the common governmental structures that the Roman Catholic Church has judged necessary to ecclesial unity. The conversations which the Pontifical Council for Promoting Christian Unity holds with "the Evangelicals" are doubtless significant in in several ways; but it may be wondered just what are the institutional or personal bodies with which the Roman Catholic Church would concretely come to the realization of ecclesial unity as a result of these conversations.[97]

Third, the transdenominational unity which Evangelicals experience with kindred spirits has a counterpart in the unity which liberal Christians share on what they call "the issues," meaning social questions and causes where traditional Christianity in all its confessional forms appears more conservative. Many of these are matters to do with sex and gender. Taking the nearest example to hand, an Associated Press report of Wednesday January 19, 2000, runs:

> NEW YORK. Dramatizing the most divisive issue in American religion, 850 mostly liberal members of the clergy and other religious figures issued a declaration Tuesday urging all faiths to bless same-sex couples and allow openly gay ministers.

Among endorsers of the statement were the retired leader of the Episcopal Church, the presidents of the United Church of Christ and Unitarian Universalist Association, presidents or deans at 15 Protestant seminaries, and numerous theology teachers.

The declaration got slim backing among Roman Catholics, and none from any major Evangelical, black Protestant, Eastern Orthodox, Mormon, Buddhist, Hindu or Muslim organizations.

Besides homosexuality, the paper advocates open access to abortion and sex education at all levels.[98]

The fact that the slender support from Catholics included "two nuns and a few lay activists" hints that one must also take care as to Catholic dialogue partners. On some issues, the dissent from official Catholic teaching would be stronger. The Roman Catholic Church has not been spared an inner turmoil in the interpretation and implementation of the Second Vatican Council.[99]

THE FUTURE

We have recorded the progress made towards reconciliation and reunion between Protestantism and the Roman Catholic Church, particularly during the second half of the twentieth century; we have noted the areas in which further doctrinal work is needed and have made a few suggestions with regard to some of them; and we have watched the emergence of some new problems. It remains now to portray with the broadest of brushes the global scene on which the story will continue to unfold in the early decades of the third millennium. I am neither a prophet nor the son of a prophet, but there are enough factors already in place for us to think that the circumstances will include (1) the continuing dechristianization of Europe, (2) a further "southward" shift in Christianity's center of gravity, and (3) growing pressure to come to terms with the (other) "world religions."

First: Europe. At the end of 1999, in an event considered worth reporting in the Raleigh *News and Observer*, the Church of Sweden ceased to be a "state church," and that in a country where until recently it seemed that 101 per cent of the population received baptism at Lutheran hands.[100] The plummeting baptismal figures of the Church of England have already been remarked on, and it has for some decades been proverbial that there are now "more Muslims than Methodists" in Britain. German universities are finding the number of faculty positions in theology cut by the regional governments. Nor have the predominantly Catholic countries of southern Europe been exempt from a decline in the Church's legal, institutional, social, and cultural influence and standing. To this must be added in eastern Europe—with the partial exception of Poland and for all the brave resistance of Christian minorities elsewhere—the long-term effects of a period of two or three generations of atheist ideology under communist regimes.

Small wonder that a persistent theme in John Paul II's pontificate has been the call for "a new evangelization of Europe." Over the same period, that theme was echoed on the Protestant side by the challenge to "a reconversion of the West" voiced by the prominent ecumenist and missiologist Bishop Lesslie Newbigin throughout his two decades of active "retirement" in Britain after thirty-five years' service in South India.[101] The "West," of course, implies the inclusion of the United States in the need for cultural reconversion (think only of the silicon elite, the media, and the literary, artistic, and educational establishments), and the problem indeed extends as far as "Western culture" reaches. Newbigin stressed both the intellectual task of addressing the culture of "advanced modernity" and the indispensable role of the local church in evangelism. On both scores, the collaboration of Catholics and Protestants—and most profoundly their unity—is surely needed, as both the Pope and Newbigin have recognized.

Secondly: the twentieth century saw the exponential growth of Christianity in sub-Saharan Africa and, more recently, in parts of Asia. From my experience as a missionary in Cameroon in the 1960s and 1970s I remember among both Catholics and Protestants not only a firm attachment to the ways they had respectively inherited from those who first brought them the Gospel but also a certain resentment at the divisions imported from the ecclesiastical West into peoples that had been culturally united. A complicating factor has been the rise and rapid spread of a multitude of "African independent churches." If Africa goes on its way to becoming "a Christian continent," it seems likely that the face of

the faith, at least, will change, and that styles of
thought, speech, ritual, and social organization will
develop that appear very strange to such Christians
as remain in the heart-lands of either Roman Catholicism or Protestantism. One can only wonder
what may be the effects of African Christianity in the
global Church.[102] Similar things might happen *mu-
tatis mutandis* in regard to Korea or even, if the
"opening up" finally occurred, China.

Thirdly: the "world religions." In different times,
places, and circumstances, the evaluations made by
Christian thinkers of (other) religions have swung
between the poles of "idolatry" and "*praeparatio
evangelica.*"[103] Besides the "exclusivists" and the
"inclusivists" there is today a camp of "pluralists"—
including, say, the Catholic Knitter and the Protestant Hick—who consider all the great religions as
paths to salvation. Evangelical Protestants typically
stress the need for explicit confession of Christ,
while contemporary Roman Catholics—resting perhaps on a long tradition of natural theology—tend
towards inclusivism. Official Catholic teaching, as
found in the Vatican II declaration *Nostra Aetate*,
sets the parameters for thinking and practice as
follows: "The Catholic Church rejects nothing of
what is true and holy in these religions. She has a
high regard for the manner of life and conduct, the
precepts and doctrines which, although differing in
many ways from her own teaching, nevertheless
often reflect a ray of that truth which enlightens all
men. Yet she proclaims and is in duty bound to
proclaim without fail Christ who is the way, the
truth and the life (Jn 14:6). In him, in whom God

reconciled all things to himself (2 Cor. 5:18-19), men find the fullness of their religious life."

Vatican II commended "dialogue," and the World Council of Churches has a long-running program of "dialogue with people of other living faiths." But much will remain in the twenty-first century to be clarified about the nature of inter-religious dialogue and its relation to evangelization. Meanwhile, WCC Faith and Order's provisional text of 1998 on *The Nature and Purpose of the Church* declares in one of its "problem boxes" that "churches today differ concerning what are the tolerable limits to diversity in confessing the one faith. For instance, is it church-dividing: to understand the resurrection of Christ only symbolically? to confess Christ only as one mediator among others?"[104] No church is named as asking whether these issues are necessarily church-dividing, but the United Church of Canada is a more likely candidate than the Roman Catholic.

*

* *

If such is the scene at the turn of the millennia, then it is high time for a reinvigoration of the ecumenical movement such as John Paul II sought to inspire in his encyclical *Ut Unum Sint*. At a time when the World Council of Churches – hitherto the chief institutional vehicle of modern ecumenism – seemed to have lost the original vision, the Pope lifted up the banner of unity in truth and life for the sake of proclaiming a credible Gospel to the entire world, and all for God's glory.[105]

That is the cue for one final raising of the question "Is the Reformation over?" There is evidence that Martin Luther understood himself as a mere "precursor of the Reformation," an evangelist whose task it was to prepare the way for the great Reformation that God alone could and would soon bring.[106] Our time again is taking on an apocalyptic hue. It is marked by at least two characteristics of biblical apocalyptic: a *universalization of horizons* is taking place as – despite all local fragmentation – we move for good or ill towards "one world"; and each and all are thereby confronted with a *critical choice* between life and death.

Jesus said: "This gospel of the kingdom will be preached throughout the whole world, as a testimony to all nations; and then the end will come" (Matthew 24:14).

NOTES

[1] The English text of the Joint Declaration is accessible in *Origins* 28/8 (July 16, 1998) 120-127, the German text in *Materialdienst des Konfessionskundlichen Instituts* 48/2 (März-April 1997) 34-37. Both versions were printed in brochures, with commentary, by the (Lutheran) Institute for Ecumenical Research at Strasbourg in 1998: *Gemeinsame Erklärung zur Rechtfertigungslehre*, and *Joint Declaration on the Doctrine of Justification*.—The phrase "articulus stantis et cadentis ecclesiae" is not found in Luther, but he comes very close to it in several places. Thus in the Commentary on Galatians of 1531-1535, he equates the "articulus iustitiae Christianae" with the "veritas Evangelii" and the "gloria Christi" (*Werke*, Weimarer Ausgabe, vol. 40/1, p. 296); and in his preface of 1537 to the doctoral disputation of Palladius, Luther calls the article on justification "the master and

prince, the lord, ruler and judge over every kind of doctrine, which conserves and governs all teaching of the Church" (WA, vol. 39/1, 205); cf. also the Smalcald articles, II.1. — Erwin Iserloh has argued that Luther never nailed the theses to the door; the event of October 31, 1517 was Luther's writing of the letter to the archbishop of Magdeburg to which he attached the theses. See *Luther zwischen Reform und Reformation: Der Thesenanschlag fand nicht statt* (Münster: Aschendorff, 1966; expanded 3rd ed. 1966); ET *The Theses Were Not Posted: Luther between Reform and Reformation* (London: Geoffrey Chapman, 1968). Iserloh gives 1668 as the year for the beginning of the annual celebration.

[2] For some account of the German debate, and some "cross-bench" observations on the original text, see my article—originally given as a lecture at the Universities of Bonn and Erlangen in May 1998—"Rechtfertigung: lutherisch oder katholisch? Überlegungen eines methodistischen Wechsel-wählers" in *Kerygma und Dogma* 45 (1999) 182-206. For the protocols of June 1999, see *Origins* 29/6 (June 24, 1999) 87-92.

[3] For the events at Augsburg on October 31, 1999, see *Origins* 29/22 (November 11, 1999) 341-348.

[4] This fact was recognized by Pope John Paul II: "The ecumenical movement really began within the churches and ecclesial communities of the Reformation" (*Ut unum sint*, 65). For my theological overview of the ecumenical movement in the twentieth century, see the Peter Ainslie Lecture on Christian Unity for 1996, "The Twentieth-Century Ecumenical Movement: The Continuing Legacy" in *Mid-Stream* 36 (1997) 119-137.

[5] Yves Congar, *Chrétiens désunis: Principes d'un "oecuménisme" catholique* (Paris: Éditions du Cerf, 1937), ET *Divided Christendom: A Catholic Study of the Problem of Reunion* (London: Geoffrey Bles, 1939).

[6] In these next five sections I shall be developing and updating a sketch I first made in a brief article, "Is the Reformation Over?" in *Theological Students Fellowship Bulletin* 7/5 (May-June 1984) 2-5.

[7] The quotation comes from an ordination address given by Archbishop Lefebvre on Jule 29, 1976. English translation in Yves Congar, *Challenge to the Church: The Case of Archbishop Lefebvre* (Huntington, Indiana: Our Sunday Visitor, 1977), 29-30.

[8] English text in *The Post-Synodal Apostolic Exhortations of John Paul II*, (ed.) J. Michael Miller (Huntington, Indiana: Our Sinday Visitor, 1998).

[9] Raleigh *News and Observer*, December 30, 1999: "Luther was responsible for the most important social/cultural/political development of the millennium, which is pluralism.... Luther's theology of justification by faith alone – rather than by the performance of preordained rituals or adherence to strict church rules – underpins even our secular ideas about the sanctity of individual conscience. But most of all, Luther (along with other figures of the Reformation) broke the monopoly of one authority to define the rules of people's inner lives."

[10] Johann Christoph Hampe, ed., *Ende der Gegenreformation? Das Konzil: Dokumente und Deutung* (Stuttgart: Kreuz-Verlag, and Mainz: Matthias-Grünewald-Verlag, 1964). The editor, himself a Protestant, notes that the "Counter-Reformation" had of course produced on the Protestant side a "Counter-Counter-Reformation" – as we shall see in a moment.

[11] See Geoffrey Wainwright, "From Word and/or Sacrament to 'Verbum Caro' = 'Mysterium Fidei': Lessons Learned from the 'BEM' Process" in Patrick Lyons, ed., *Parola e sacramento* (Roma: Ponteficio Ateneo S. Anselmo, 1997), 141-175.

[12] For a historical study critical of the practice, see Robert Taft, "Communion via Intinction" in *Studia Liturgica* 26 (1996) 225-236.

[13] Vittorio Subilia, *La nuova cattolicità del Cattolicesimo: una valutazione protestante del Concilio Vaticano Secondo* (Torino: Claudiana, 1967); see already *Il problema del Cattolicesimo* (Torino: Claudiana, 1962).

[14] Vittorio Subilia, *Tempo di confessione e di rivoluzione* (Torino: Claudiana, 1968), 147-151, and *La giustificazione per fede* (Brescia: Paideia, 1976), 318-322.

[15] Maximin Piette, *La réaction wesléyenne dans l'évolution protestante* (Bruxelles: La Lecture au Foyer, 1925); ET *John Wesley in the Evolution of Protestantism* (New York: Sheed & Ward, 1937).

[16] See Geoffrey Wainwright, "Word and Sacrament in the Churches' Responses to the Lima Text" in *One in Christ* 24 (1988) 304-327. The original text of *Baptism, Eucharist and Ministry* was published as Faith and Order Paper No. 111 (Geneva: World Council of Churches, 1982).

[17] *Churches Respond to BEM: Official Responses to the "Baptism, Eucharist and Ministry" Text*, vol. 2, ed. Max Thurian (Geneva: World Council of Churches, 1986), 70-71.

[18] *Baptism, Eucharist and Ministry 1982-1990*, Faith and Order Paper No. 149 (Geneva: WCC, 1990), 110-11.

[19] André Birmelé, *Le salut en Jésus-Christ dans les dialogues oecuméniques* (Paris: Éditions du Cerf, and Geneva: Labor et Fides, 1986), 249-253. See also the more popular study book produced by Birmelé and the Catholic theologian Thomas Ruster, *Alleinseligmachend? Das Thema Kirche im Gespäch der Kirchen* (Würzburg: Echter, and Göttingen: Vandenhoeck & Ruprecht, 1988). The U.S. meeting of Evangelicals and Catholics in 1994 described the difference as "the Church as an integral part of the Gospel" (Catholic) *versus* "the Church as a communal consequence of the Gospel" (Evangelical); see "Evangelicals and Catholics Together: The Christian Mission in the Third Millennium" in *First Things* no. 43 (May 1994) 15-22, esp. 17.

[20] See already the Report of the Third Phase of the Lutheran / Catholic International Dialogue, "Church and Justification: Understanding the Church in the light of the Doctrine of Justification" in *Pontifical Council for Promoting Christian Unity: Information Service* no. 86 (1994/2-3) 128-188.

[21] Joseph Lortz, *Die Reformation in Deutschland*, 2 vols. (Freiburg im Breisgau: Herder, 1939-40); ET *The Reformation in Germany* (London: Darton, Longman & Todd, and New York: Herder, 1968).

[22] Francis Clark, *Eucharistic Sacrifice and the Reformation* (Oxford: Blackwell, 1960; 2nd ed. 1967).

[23] Nicholas Lash, *His Presence in the World: A Study in Eucharistic Worship and Theology* (London: Sheed & Ward, 1968), 127f.

[24] J. F. McCue, "Luther and Roman Catholicism on the mass as sacrifice," *Journal of Ecumenical Studies* 2 (1965) 205-233.

[25] Hans Küng, *Rechtfertigung: Die Lehre Karl Barths und eine katholische Besinnung* (Einsiedeln: Johannes-Verlag, 1957); ET *Justification: The Doctrine of Karl Barth and a Catholic Reflection* (Philadelphia: Westminster Press, 1964; new ed. 1981).

[26] Otto Hermann Pesch, *Hinführung zu Luther* (Mainz: Matthias-Grünewald-Verlag, 1982), 116-133, 154-175.

[27] In his fundamental work, *Die Theologie der Rechtfertigung bei Luther und Thomas von Aquin: Versuch eines systematisch-theologischen Dialogs* (Mainz: Matthias- Grünewald-Verlag, 1967), Pesch had drawn a disctinction between the *sapiential* theologizing of Thomas Aquinas and the *existential* theologizing of Martin Luther. *Doxologically*, we ascribe all the work to God; but *on reflection*, we come to see that God also enables *us to work*. That, of course, raises the question of the proper relations between worship and doctrine.

[28] The "annex" was able to produce from a Lutheran confessional document a case of the language of "cooperation" used in a mutually acceptable way *when once a person has been "converted"*: "As soon as the Holy Spirit has initiated his work of regeneration and renewal in us through the Word and the holy sacraments, it is certain that we can and must cooperate by the power of the Holy Spirit"—so the Formula of Concord, Solid Declaration II, 64-65, found in *Die Bekenntnisschriften der evangelisch-lutherischen Kirche* (Göttingen: Vandenhoeck & Ruprecht, 1930), 897-8.

[29] Yves Congar, *Martin Luther, sa foi, sa réforme* (Paris: Éditions du Cerf, 1983), 15-83.

[30] Otto Hermann Pesch, "Der 'lutherische' Luther—eine katholische Möglichkeit?" in P. Manns and H. Meyer, eds., *Ökumenische Erschliessung Martin Luthers* (Paderborn: Bonifatius-Druckerei, and Frankfurt am Main: Otto-Lembeck-Verlag, 1983), 44-66; ET *Luther's Ecumenical*

Significance: An Interconfessional Consultation (Philadelphia: Fortress Press, 1984), 27-45.

[31] See the contributions of Erwin Iserloh and Peter Manns to the book mentioned in the previous note.

[32] O. H. Pesch, *Hinführung zu Luther* (1982); Peter Manns, inaugural address at the Institute for European History, Mainz, in 1981 ("Vater im Glauben"); Jan Willebrands, address to the Lutheran World Federation at Evian in 1970 (text in *Herder-Korrespondenz* 24 [1970] 427-431).

[33] George A. Lindbeck, *The Nature of Doctrine: Religion and Theology in a Postliberal Age* (Philadelphia: Westminster Press, 1984).

[34] Ibid., 15.

[35] Ibid., 18.

[36] Ibid., 96.

[37] Ibid., 97.

[38] Heinrich Fries and Karl Rahner, *Einigung der Kirche—reale Möglichkeit* (Freiburg im Breisgau: Herder, 1983); ET *Unity of the Churches–An Actual Possibility* (Philadelphia: Fortress Press, and New York: Paulist Press, 1985). The translations in the text above are my own.

[39] J. R. Geiselmann, "Das Konzil von Trient über das Verhältnis der Heiligen Schrift und der nicht geschriebenen Traditionen" in M. Schmaus (ed.), *Die mündliche Über-lieferung* (München: Max-Hueber-Verlag, 1957), 123-206; cf. Y. Congar, *La Tradition et les Traditions*, 2 vols. (Paris: Éditions Arthème Fayard, 1960-63), ET *Tradition and Traditions* (New York: Macmillan, 1967).

[40] See *The Fourth World Conference on Faith and Order, Montreal 1963*, Faith and Order Paper No. 42, P. C. Rodger and L. Vischer, eds. (New York: Association Press, 1964), pp. 50-61.

[41] See *Baptism, Eucharist and Ministry*, Faith and Order Paper No. 111 (Geneva: WCC, 1982), and *Baptism, Eucharist and Ministry 1982-1990: Report on the Process and Responses*, Faith and Order Paper No. 149 (Geneva: WCC, 1990); and *Confessing the One Faith: An Ecumenical Explication of the Apostolic Faith as it is Confessed in the Nicene-Constantin-opolitan Creed (381)*, Faith and Order Paper No. 153 (Geneva: WCC, 1991).

[42] Max Thurian, *L'Eucharistie – Mémorial du Seigneur, Sacrifice d'action de grâce et d'intercession* (Neuchâtel: Delachaux & Niestlé 1959); ET *The Eucharistic Memorial*, 2 vols. (Richmond: John Knox Press, 1961).

[43] *Towards Visible Unity: Commission on Faith and Order, Lima 1982*, volume 1: Minutes and Addresses, Faith and Order Paper No. 112 (Geneva: WCC, 1982), 80-84.

[44] *Baptism, Eucharist and Ministry 1982-1990*, 115f.

[45] See Geoffrey Wainwright, "The Eucharist in the Churches' Responses to the Lima Text" in *One in Christ* 25 (19889) 53-74, esp. 53-54, 56-58, and accompanying end-notes. For the Roman Catholic response, see *Churches Respond to BEM*, vol. 6, Max Thurian, ed. (Geneva: WCC, 1988), 1-40, esp. 22-23.

[46] For the Roman Catholic response, see *Churches Respond to BEM*, vol. 6, 19-21. For a listing of the Protestant responses where reservations are expressed concerning sacrifice, see my article mentioned in the previous note, in particular p. 69, note 10.

[47] See Irmgard Pahl, "The Paschal Mystery in its Central Meaning for the Shape of Christian Liturgy" in *Studia Liturgica* 26 (1996) 16-38.

[48] A. R. George, *Communion with God in the New Testament* (London: Epworth Press, 1953); J. Zizioulas, *Being as Communion Studies in Personhood and the Church* (Crestwood, New York: St. Vladimir's Seminary Press, 1985). See G. Wainwright, "The Doctrine of the Trinity: Where the Church Stands or Falls" in *Interpretation* 45 (1991) 117-132, and "The Ecumenical Rediscovery of the Trinity" in *One in Christ* 34 (1998) 95-124.

[49] Thomas F. Best and Günther Gassmann, eds., *On the Way to Fuller Communion: Official Report of the Fifth World Conference on Faith and Order, Santiago de Compostela 1993*, Faith and Order Paper No. 166 (Geneva: WCC, 1994).

[50] So *Lumen Gentium*, 4, summarizing the trinitarian opening of the document. The reference in Cyprian is *De oratione dominca* 23 (PL 4, 553): "… de unitate Patris, et Filii, et Spiritus sancti, plebs adunata."

[51] *Unitatis Redintegratio*, 2.

[52] See *The Ecumenical Review* 36 (1984), 259. I have italicized the word *fellowship* because it long figured in Protestant English usage at least as a translation of *koinônia*. The word "communion" has largely gained a monopoly more recently, perhaps because some hear a sexist ring to "fellowship" and perhaps in deference to the lingering Latinity of Roman Catholic usage.

[53] G. Wainwright, "The Nature of Communion," in *Ecumenical Trends* 28/6 (June 1998) 1-8 (81-88).

[54] See G. Wainwright, "The Church as Communion: A Methodist Response" in *Catholic International* 3, No. 16 (1-30 September 1992), 769-771.

[55] Jean-Jacques von Allmen, "L'Église locale parmi les autres Eglises locales" in *Irénikon* 43 (1970) 512-537: "Une Église locale est entièrement Église, mais elle n'est pas toute l'Église. See also the book by this same insightful and imaginative theologian who personal and literary influence I gladly acknowledge, *La primauté de l'Église de Pierre et de Paul: Remarques d'un protestant* (Fribourg-en-Suisse: Éditions Universitaires, and Paris: Éditions du Cerf, 1977).

[56] See the studies edited by Raymond E. Brown and others, *Peter in the New Testament* (Minneapolis: Augsburg Press, and New York: Paulist Press, 1973) and *Mary in the New Testament* (Minneapolis: Augsburg Press, and New York: Paulist Press, 1978).

[57] *Towards a Statement on the Church*, paragraphs 41-47, here paragraph 47. When, in the Commission, we were looking for an adjective in the phrase that became "a *weak* human being," I proposed "fallible"; this suggestion provoked immediate general laughter but did not find final acceptance.

[58] Walter Klaiber, "Die Einheit der Kirche und der Wille Gottes: Evangelisch-methodistisches Positionspapier zum Gespräch über den Primat des Papstes" in *Theologische Quartalschrift* 178 (1998) 131-140.

[59] *Mary in the New Testament*, esp. 279-280, 283, 288-289, 294.

[60] See G. Wainwright, *The Ecumenical Moment: Crisis and Opportunity for the Church* (Grand Rapids: Eerdmans, 1983)

169-188 (a chapter which reproduces an article of mine from *One in Christ* 11 [1975] 121-144).

[61] *Ut Unum Sint*, 79.

[62] This cluster of themes was treated in four of the volumes in the national series of "Lutherans and Catholics in Dialogue" (numbers 1, 5, 6, and 9): *The Status of the Nicene Creed as Dogma of the Church*, (U. S. National Committee of the Lutheran World Federation and the Roman Catholic Bishops' Commission for Ecumenical Affairs, 1965); *Papal Primacy and the Universal Church*, ed. P. C. Empie and T. A. Murphy (Minneapolis: Augsburg Press, 1974); *Teaching Authority and Infallibility in the Church*, ed. P. C. Empie, T. A. Murphy, and J. A. Burgess (Minneapolis: Augsburg Press, 1980); *Scripture and Tradition*, ed. H. C. Skillrud, J. F. Stafford, and D. F. Martensen (Minneapolis: Augsburg, 1995).

[63] "Kirchengeschichte als Geschichte der Auslegung der Heiligen Schrift" (inaugural lecture at Tübingen, 1946), reprinted in Gerhard Ebeling, *Wort Gottes und Tradition: Studien zu einer Hermeneutik für Konfessionen* (Göttingen; Vandenhoeck & Ruprecht, 2nd ed. 1966), 9-27.

[64] "Quel est le sens de la Réforme dans le plan de Dieu?" See Yves Congar, *Martin Luther, sa foi, sa réforme* (Paris: Éditions du Cerf, 1983), p. 7.

[65] See Geoffrey Wainwright, "Towards an Ecumenical Hermeneutic: How Can All Christians Read the Scriptures Together?" in *Gregorianum* 76 (1995) 639-662. At the beginning of the contemporary retrieval of earlier approaches to the Bible stands the great work of Henri de Lubac, *Exégèse médiévale*, 4 vols. (Paris: Aubier-Montaigne, 1959-64), now in process of translation and publication with Eerdmans: *Medieval Exegesis*, vol. 1: *The Four Senses of Scripture* (1998). One may now add Thomas F. Torrance, *Divine Meaning: Studies in Patristic Hermeneutics* (Edinburgh: T. & T. Clark, 1995), and Frances M. Young, *Biblical Exegesis and the Formation of Christian Culture* (Cambridge University Press, 1997). Two of my doctoral students have written their dissertations on the history of the interpretation of portions of Scripture: W. Ellison Jones, "The Feeding of the Multi-

tude: A Theological Analysis of the History of its Interpretation" (Ph. D. dissertation, Duke University, 1997) and Margaret Kim Peterson "Psalm 8: A Theological and Historical Analysis of its Interpretation" (Ph. D. dissertation, Duke University, 1998). Another, William T. Flynn, opened up a new track in *Medieval Music as Medieval Exegesis* (Lanhham, Maryland: Scarecrow Press, 1999).

[66] See Horace T. Allen, *On Common Ground: The Story of the Revised Common Lectionary* (Norwich, England: Canterbury Press, 1998).

[67] Historical studies on the proclamation of the Word in the liturgical assembly in the great Tradition are found in H. O. Old, *The Reading and Preaching of the Scriptures in the Worship of the Christian Church*, vol. 1, *The Biblical Period* (Grand Rapids: Eerdmans, 1998); vol. 2, *The Patristic Age* (1998); vol. 3, *The Medieval Church* (1999)

[68] *Baptism, Eucharist and Ministry 1982-1990*, 117. I have to confess that not only was I closely involved in the work on *BEM* leading up to Lima but also in monitoring the responses from the churches and in composing the synthesizing report of the process in 1990.

[69] *Baptism, Eucharist and Ministry 1992-1990*, p. 118.

[70] cf. *BEM*, M 39, which the Roman Catholic response recognized as a description of ordination "consonant with the faith and the practice of the Catholic Church" (*Churches Respond to BEM*, vol. 6, 33).

[71] *Pastores dabo vobis* (1992), 12.4, and 23.2. English text in *The Post-Synodal Apostolic Exhortations of John Paul II*, J. Michael Miller, ed. (Huntington, Indiana: Our Sunday Visitor, 1998).

[72] *Churches Respond to BEM*, vol. 6, 33.

[73] Geoffrey Wainwright, "Is Episcopal Succession a Matter of Dogma for Anglicans? The Evidence of Some Recent Dialogues" in Colin Podmore, ed., *Community, Unity, Communion: Essays in Honour of Mary Tanner* (London: Church House Publishing, 1998), 164-179.

[74] See, for example, *Baptism, Eucharist and Ministry*, M 34, and the 1991 report of the Methodist-Catholic international dialogue, *The Apostolic Tradition*; cf. already the 1963

Montreal text of Faith and Order, "Scripture, Tradition, and traditions," mentioned earlier.

[75] Harding Meyer, " 'Suprema auctoritatis ideo ab omne errore immunis': The Lutheran Approach to Primacy" in James F. Puglisi, ed., *Petrine Ministry and the Unity of the Church* (Collegeville, Minnesota: Liturgical Press, 1999) 15-34.

[76] Geoffrey Wainwright, "'The Gift Which He on One Bestows, We All Delight to Prove': A Possible Methodist Approach to a Ministry of Primacy in the Circulation of Truth and Love" in *Petrine Ministry and the Unity of the Church*, pp. 59-82, esp. 82.

[77] G. Osborn, ed., *The Poetical Works of John and Charles Wesley* (London: Wesleyan-Methodist Conference Office, 1868-72), vol. 4 (1869), 108, and vol. 7 (1870), 81.

[78] "Maria—Typus der Kirche und Typus der Menschheit" in Lukas Vischer, *Ökumenische Skizzen* (Frankfurt am Main: Verlag Otto Lembeck, 1972), 109-123.

[79] That this is an appropriate configuration of topics is confirmed by the approach taken in volume 8 of the national series of "Lutherans and Catholics in Dialogue": *The One Mediator, the Saints, and Mary*, H. G. Anderson, J. F. Stafford, and J. A Burgess, eds. (Minneapolis: Augsburg Press, 1992).

[80] Edward Schillebeeckx, *Mary, Mother of the Redemption* (London: Sheed & Ward, 1964), 122. The English translation contains revisions and additions to the earlier Dutch, *Maria, Moeder van de verlossing*.

[81] When, in 1997, rumors were circulating in the public prints concerning a possible formal papal definition of Mary as co-redemptrix, it was comforting to learn that a specially appointed commission of distinguished mariologists had recently discountenanced such a move.

[82] The writer of the booklet was the Roman Catholic priest Michael Evans. The present writer is pleased to note that many of the connections and correspondences made with Methodist doctrine had been adumbrated in his own text on "Mary and Methodism" mentioned earlier.

[83] See *One in Christ* 28 (1992) 89-90.

[84] See the Lutheran-Catholic text, *The One Mediator, the Saints, and Mary* (1992).

[85] For surrounding arguments, see Geoffrey Wainwright, *Methodists in Dialogue* (Nashville: Abingdon Press, 1995), 237-249 ("Wesley and the Communion of Saints").

[86] See *Towards a Common Understanding of the Church: Reformed / Roman Catholic International Dialogue, Second Phase, 1984-1990* (Geneva: World Alliance of Reformed Churches, 1991).

[87] *Life in Christ: Morals, Communion and the Church* (London: Church House Publishing, and Catholic Truth Society, 1994), 1 (paragraph 1), 20-32 (paragraphs 54-88).

[88] Reinhard Hütter and Theodor Dieter, eds., *Ecumenical Ventures in Ethics: Protestants Engage Pope John Paul II's Moral Encyclicals* (Grand Rapids: Eerdmans, 1998).

[89] See, for instance, George Weigel, *Witness to Hope The Biography of Pope John Paul II* (New York: Harper Collins, 1999), 518-522.

[90] Apostolic letter, *Ordinatio Sacerdotalis*, 2-3. See *Origins* 24/4 (June 9, 1994) 49-52, esp. 51.

[91] See *Vatican Council II: More Postconciliar Documents*, ed. Austin Flannery (Grand Rapids: Eerdmans, 1982), 331-345, esp. 339-40.

[92] *Ordinatio Sacerdotalis*, 3, in *Origins* 24/4, 51.

[93] Geoffrey Wainwright, *The Ecumenical Moment: Crisis and Opportunity for the Church* (Grand Rapids: Eerdmans, 1983), 189.

[94] Dietrich Bonhoeffer, *No Rusty Swords: Letters, Lectures and Notes 1928-1936* (New York: Harper and Row, 1965), 92-118.

[95] Figures from the respective editions of the *Yearbook of American and Canadian Churches*.

[96] See *First Things* no. 43 (May 1994), 15-22 ("Evangelicals and Catholics Together: The Christian Mission in the Third Millennium"), and no. 79 (January 1998), 20-23 ("The Gift of Salvation").

[97] The Chicago Lutheran pastor Frank Senn has imagined Rome putting in place an "Evangelical Rite" as a structure to welcome such Lutherans, Anglicans, Reformed, and

Methodists as desire to "come home," while retaining a spiritual and liturgical "style"—and even episcopate—of their own. The nearest precedent would seem to be, as Senn himself recognizes, the "uniate" relation of the Eastern Catholic Churches to Rome. See the discussion in *Lutheran Forum* 28/4 (Advent / November 1994), 8 (Senn); 33/1 (Easter / Spring 1999), 22-28 (Maxwell E. Johnson); 33/3 (Una Sancta / Fall 1999), 6 and 52 (Senn).

[98] Raleigh *News and Observer*, January 19, 2000, 5A. The report goes on to say that "nine bishops and a dozen seminary professors gave endorsements from the Episcopal Church, which will vote on same-sex rituals in July," and that "among Catholics, support came from two nuns and a few lay activists."

[99] See George Weigel, *Witness to Hope: The Biography of John Paul II*, passim. Weigel credits Pope John Paul with having done much to settle the turmoil by dint of an authentic and consistent reading and application. Following a very positive review of Weigel's book by Owen Chadwick in *The Times Literary Supplement* of December 24, 1999, letters apparently from two liberal Catholics in the *TLS* of January 14, 2000, claim that John Paul "is a man who will leave a Church considerably more ill at ease with itself and deeply divided than when he found it, and after whose demise it will probably self-destruct" (Dominic Kirkham), a Pope who "has undone much of the good that the Vatican Council achieved … and has driven the Church to the brink of moral and intellectual, and perhaps, at the next papal election, institutional suicide" (Norman F. Cantor).

[100] *Raleigh News and Observer*, December 28, 1999: "After nearly five centuries as the state church, Lutheranism will end its ties with the Swedish government on New Year's Day and will be treated like any other religion. 'It's a happy separation—or a happy divorce—that has evolved over many years, and that is very good,' said Carl-Einar Nordling of the Ministry of Culture. 'Swedish society has outgrown the state church system. The state church system is founded on the ideology of "one country, one people, one ruler." You only have to say that to feel how foreign it is in today's

society.' Although 90 percent of Swedes nominally are Lutheran, the change reflects demographic and immigration trends as well as Swedes' general indifference to organized religion." Some put Sunday church attendance figutes at one percent.

[101] See Geoffrey Wainwright, *Lesslie Newbigin: A Theological Life* (New York and Oxford: Oxford University Press, forthcoming 2000).

[102] See Geoffrey Wainwright, "Christianity in (South) Africa: Ecumenical Challenges in the Twenty-First Century," forthcoming in *Nederduitse gereformeerde teologiese tydskrif.*

[103] For a historical survey see Julien Ries, *Les chrétiens parmi les religions: Des "Actes des Apôtres" à Vatican II* (Paris: Desclée, 1987).

[104] *The Nature and Purpose of the Church: A Stage on the Way to a Common Statement*, Faith and Order Paper No. 181 (Geneva: WCC, 1998), 36.

[105] At the end of the Canberra Assembly of the WCC in 1991, Orthodox and Evangelical participants summoned the institution to return to its own doctrinal basis in the Scriptures; see *Signs of the Times: Official Report, Seventh Assembly, Canberra, Australia, 7-20 February 1991*, Michael Kinnamon, ed. (Geneva: WCC, and Grand Rapids: Eerdmans, 1991), 279-286. For my criticism of the "paradigm shift" that the current general secretary of the WCC, Konrad Raiser, saw as beginning in 1968 and has tried to further, see *Mid-Stream* 31 (1992) 169-173. It is a sad irony that the WCC should have started – from the Uppsala assembly of 1968 onwards—to lose its original commitment to redemptive history so soon after the Roman Catholic Church, with Vatican II, had entered an ecumenical movement that it understood in precisely that salvation-historical way.

[106] See Heiko A. Oberman, "Martin Luther – Vorläufer der Reformation" in *Verifikationen: Festschrift für Gerhard Ebeling zum 70. Geburtstag*, (eds.) E. Jüngel , J. Wallmann and W. Werbeck (Tübingen: Mohr-Siebeck, 1982), 91-119; see also Oberman's book, *Luther: Mensch zwischen Gott und Teufel* (Berlin: Severin & Siedler, 1982).

THE PÈRE MARQUETTE LECTURES IN THEOLOGY

1969 *The Authority for Authority*
  Quentin Quesnell
    Marquette University

1970 *Mystery and Truth*
  John Macquarrie
    Union Theological Seminary

1971 *Doctrinal Pluralism*
  Bernard Lonergan, S.J.
    Regis College, Ontario

1972 *Infallibility*
  George A. Lindbeck
    Yale University

1973 *Ambiguity in Moral Choice*
  Richard A. McCormick, S.J.
    Bellarmine School of Theology

1974 *Church Membership as a Catholic and Ecumenical Problem*
  Avery Dulles, S.J.
    Woodstock College

1975 *The Contributions of Theology to Medical Ethics*
  James Gustafson
    University of Chicago

1976 *Religious Values in an Age of Violence*
  Rabbi Marc Tannenbaum
    Director of National Interreligious Affairs
    American Jewish Committee, New York City

1977 *Truth Beyond Relativism: Karl Mannheim's Sociology of
      Knowledge*
  Gregory Baum
    St. Michael's College

1978 *A Theology of 'Uncreated Energies'*
　　　George A. Maloney, S.J.
　　　　John XXIII Center for Eastern Christian Studies
　　　　Fordham University

1980 *Method in Theology: An Organon For Our Time*
　　　Frederick E. Crowe, S.J.
　　　　Regis College, Toronto

1981 *Catholics in the Promised Land of the Saints*
　　　James Hennesey, S.J.
　　　　Boston College

1982 *Whose Experience Counts in Theological Reflection?*
　　　Monika Hellwig
　　　　Georgetown University

1983 *The Theology and Setting of Discipleship in the Gospel of Mark*
　　　John R. Donahue, S.J.
　　　　Jesuit School of Theology, Berkeley

1984 *Should War be Eliminated? Philosophical and Theological Investigations*
　　　Stanley Hauerwas
　　　　Notre Dame University

1985 *From Vision to Legislation: From the Council to a Code of Laws*
　　　Ladislas M. Orsy, S.J.
　　　　The Catholic University of America

1986 *Revelation and Violence: A Study in Contextualization*
　　　Walter Brueggemann
　　　　Eden Theological Seminary
　　　　St. Louis, Missouri

1987 *Nova et Vetera: The Theology of Tradition in American
        Catholicism*
        Gerald Fogarty
        University of Virginia

1988 *The Christian Understanding of Freedom and the History
        of Freedom in the Modern Era: The Meeting and Confron-
        tation Between Christianity and the Modern Era in a
        Postmodern Situation*
        Walter Kasper
        University of Tübingen

1989 *Moral Absolutes: Catholic Tradition, Current Trends, and
        the Truth*
        William F. May
        Catholic University of America

1990 *Is Mark's Gospel a Life of Jesus? The Question of Genre*
        Adela Yarbro Collins
        University of Notre Dame

1991 *Faith, History and Cultures: Stability and Change in
        Church Teachings*
        Walter H. Principe, C.S.B.
        University of Toronto

1992 *Universe and Creed*
        Stanley L. Jaki
        Seton Hall University

1993 *The Resurrection of Jesus Christ: Some Contemporary Issues*
        Gerald G. O'Collins, S.J.
        Gregorian Pontifical University

1994 *Seeking God in Contemporary Culture*
        Most Reverend Rembert G. Weakland, O.S.B.
        Archbishop of Milwaukee

About the Père Marquette Lecture Series

The Annual Père Marquette Lecture Series began at Marquette University in the Spring of 1969. Ideal for classroom use, library additions, or private collections, the Père Marquette Lecture Series has received international acceptance by scholars, universities, and libraries. Hardbound in blue cloth with gold stamped covers. Uniform style and price ($15 each). Some reprints with soft covers. Regular reprinting keeps all volumes available. Ordering information (purchase orders, checks, and major credit cards accepted):

Book Masters Distribution Services
  1444 U.S. Route 42
  P.O. Box 388
  Ashland OH 44903

Order Toll-Free (800) 247-6553
  fax: (419) 281 6883

Editorial Address:
  Dr. Andrew Tallon, Director
  Marquette University Press
  Box 1881
  Milwaukee WI 53201-1881

phone:	(414) 288-7298
fax:	(414) 288-3300
internet:	andrew.tallon@marquette.edu
web:	www.marquette.edu/mupress/

ISBN 0-87462-580-7

51500

9 780874 625806